Dreyer in Double Reflection

Translation of Carl Th. Dreyer's writings
About the Film (Om Filmen)
Edited and with accompanying commentary and essays
by Donald Skoller

 **A Dutton Paperback**

E. P. Dutton & Co., Inc. | New York | 1973

Dreyer in Double Reflection

DONALD SKOLLER received his Ph.D. in cinema and theatre from New York University. He has taught film at Hunter College, and U.C.L.A., and is currently Associate Professor of Speech and Theatre and Coordinator of the Picker Film Institute of the Davis Center for Performing Arts at the City College of New York. He has published numerous articles on film aesthetics in *Film Comment, Cinema Journal, Film Society Review,* and *Cinema,* and is currently working on new books called *Experiencing Dreyer* and *Cinematic Consciousness.*

I cannot dedicate Dreyer's writings, but whatever work went into the translation, the editing, and the commentaries I wish to dedicate to those who shared the experience most closely: my wife Eleanor, my children, friends, and parents.

Thanks go to the Danish Film Museum, especially those responsible for the vast collection of photographs from which I chose most of the stills appearing in this book.

Contents

page

List of Illustrations

Dreyer in Double Reflection

Introduction

Carl Th. Dreyer's films have a quiet inner unity, a fine weave working within and upon itself. His films achieve their intensity without high-pressuring the viewer, without being hyperactive, and it is not unusual for their strengths to go virtually unnoticed until you suddenly catch a glimpse of something coming from their center and then really begin to listen to and look at it all.

This is true not only of his films but of his writings about film as well. The essays contained in this collection cover a period of forty years, from 1920 to 1960. They are presented chronologically—rather than by subject category or some other device—because they add up to a *biographia cinematica,* one of the more interesting and illuminating on record. The individual pieces are like entries in a public diary, an artist's log covering four decades of dynamic interaction with the growing film culture of the twentieth century. They are the words and thoughts of a man who lived for film—in Dreyer's own phrase, "my only great passion"—and spoke and wrote with consistently revelatory insight and conviction. What he said and wrote always tells us something about himself at the very least and, therefore, inevitably, about the history and nature of the art to which he devoted his life.

Dreyer's last three great films—*Day of Wrath* (1943),[1] *Ordet* (1955), and *Gertrud* (1964)—were based upon stage plays, and if one includes the ill-fated *Two Lives* (1945), which also came from the theatre, his predilection for "adaptation" becomes more marked. This is sometimes pointed out by unsympathetic critics to support the contention that Dreyer's work grew less and less cinematic after his final silent film, *La Passion de Jeanne d'Arc* (*The Passion of Joan of Arc,* 1928). But to other viewers the later films

[1] In every instance, the date following a film's title is that of its first showing.

are his most cinematic, suggesting that Dreyer was drawn to material that had already been shaped dramatically in order to concentrate on further distillation and transformation of the action's most essential elements into specifically cinematic form. This sense of a director deliberately reducing his areas of concern but intent upon total realization of the remaining basic elements is consistently reflected in Dreyer's writings. The growth and refinement of this unique directorial sensibility, throughout the four decades covered, can be followed in these pages.

In Dreyer's writing about cinema, the reader is exposed to the same problems and possibilities of communication his films themselves present. And it is not unfair—perhaps even helpful—to add that these are not Dreyer's problems, not *his* transmission difficulties, but problems of reception. Of all filmmakers, Dreyer has given more than has been received. The reception difficulties likely to be encountered in Dreyer's articles and essays grow out of the same simplicity and directness characteristic of his films, the same lack of *hype*. He seems to be saying things we've heard before, sometimes things familiar to our ears, just as his images on screen seem familiar, simple, and direct, without the sense of explosion or collision that snaps its fingers in front of one's nose to adrenalate an essentially dead situation. However, in coming upon "the familiar," we have options: on the one hand, there is the *stock response,* by which we perceive just enough (and no more) of the immediately present information to trigger a past, stored reaction—in which case what is actually on screen (or page) is quite rightly experienced as a kind of regurgitation. (But *whose?*) On the other hand, "the familiar" may provide an opportunity for making further distinctions, refining perceptions—discovering what is essential. If the work in question is "familiar" in the sense of being *stale,* then nothing will really help. But many times, one can tune past surface familiarity into highly distilled images or thoughts vibrant on their own wavelengths.

Dreyer cherished the possibility of communicating. Rather than present something that could not express just what he wanted, he would not present it at all. If the odds or obstacles against doing it his way were very great, he would defy them and do it as he felt it must be done, even if this lessened his chances to work again. Once he found his own voice as a filmmaker, Dreyer became disinterested in stepping-stones. He seemed to know that the decisive moment for the artist was always the moment at hand. Compromise not only changes the work of art for all time but the artist as well. Because he was an uncompromising artist, he gave us films like *The Passion of Joan of Arc* (1928), *Vampyr* (1932), *Day of Wrath* (1943), *Ordet* (*The Word*, 1955), and *Gertrud* (1964). He also gave but then took back *Two Lives,* completed in Sweden in 1945 and later withdrawn by Dreyer himself when he became convinced that he had not really been able to overcome miscastings forced upon him by the producers. In his last years, at the very height of his development and refinement as a filmmaker, it was impossible for Dreyer to raise the money to make *Jesus,* which existed in three hundred pages of scenario (written by Dreyer in Independence, Missouri, in 1949/50); *Medea,* in which he planned to apply the color-theories he had pondered for many years; and, most tantalizing, a film version of William Faulkner's *Light in August,* which he had hoped to make in the United States. These were heavy losses for Dreyer to absorb and heavy losses for those who would like more than the last five classic films that he managed to complete after coming into his own. But Dreyer's attitude wasn't arbitrarily stubborn about these things. Rather, it was his way of protecting one of the most essential qualities upon which his work was based and which, in turn and at a certain distance, informed the special relationship to his audience so necessary for proper reception of these works: a *trust,* which he could not betray. Only within this unspoken covenant of complete mutual regard did Dreyer expect to be taken fully at his word, image, or sound. Dreyer clearly understood that his visions were so subtle and individualistic, so radically low key, that any betrayal or compromise would throw the viewer off the track and preclude the immersion and saturation of consciousness that he himself recognized as the most essential movement and aim of his style.

It is important to notice carefully the specific nature of Dreyer's remarks throughout these essays when he refers to *the effect of the image upon the viewer's mind.* When he speaks of *penetrating deeply into the spectator's consciousness,* or of *tuning the mind in a light way* through the direct impact of what the director has allowed to reach the screen, he does this in a way that affirms quite explicitly the existence of a plastic imagination, a human faculty directly and deeply responsive to all degrees and nuances of visual phenomena. One might be tempted, out of habit, to assume that his words are being used casually (as, out of habit, his apparently simple pictures are taken on the screen). This would be missing the point, missing why he has written and why he has made films. Within the reduced area of his concern, Dreyer not only touches the heart of the matter but also means everything he says exactly the way he says it.

Because this is true, special care has been taken to translate these writings with minimal loss of nuance and overtone. Encountering difficulties in a first attempt at translation, particularly with regard to connotation and denotation of words and phrases, I commissioned two additional translations of the entire text of *Om Filmen* (1959), the original collection of Dreyer's writings in Danish edited by Erik Ulrichsen. I asked Gwen Morgan, a Scandinavian linguistic scientist living in the United States, to render a translation that would be as completely *literal* (from the Danish) as even marginal coherency would allow it to be. I asked Mari-Louise Penchoen, a Dane who has lived in France and the United States during the past decade doing graduate studies in English literature, to render a translation with a heavy bias toward the colloquial possibilities of her native language. Mrs. Morgan and Mrs. Penchoen worked independently. They did not even meet until each of their versions was completed. At that point, I ended a two-year stay in Los Angeles (where the translation had been begun), returned to New York, and began the final collation and synthesis based upon their work and my own. The final result is published here, and I must take full responsibility for anything that looks odd to either of these ladies or to anyone else. The overriding principle has been to carry over the spirit of Dreyer, as well as the letter, from his native language to this one. It has been suggested that I could have *refined* certain characteristics of Dreyer's way with words more than I actually have done. I have opted—strenuously —for unpasteurized Dreyer, Dreyer with husk and kernel, unbleached, straight from the oven without cellophane wrappings. Automatic Anglicization or Americanization have been given lower priority than, for example, maintenance of the rhythms and phoneticisms shading the meaning of Dreyer's lines. These leave, or possibly even create, some awkwardnesses, but I find greater compensation in certain fresh awarenesses that result. For instance, the Danish expression "to jump over where the fence is lowest" has a more recognizable equivalent in the English "to take the line of least resistance," but, in this case, taking that line of least resistance would have deprived the reader of a delightful and more evocative expression. Some of the most gratifying results were decisions that were distilled over many months, even small things like suddenly realizing that "faldt" (as used in "To Skuespil, der faldt") was to "flop" or "fold" even more than "fall" or "fail," when it referred to quickly closed stage plays. And, at the risk of making Dreyer sound *anachronistically hip,* I settled on translating "haengende i fotografiet" directly as "hung up on photography," when Dreyer was admonishing against pictorialism for its own sake back in the early fifties. Also, it is not just with tongue in cheek that I add, at this moment, that in doing this we arrive at a deeper truth: *Dreyer has always been and continues to be anachronistically hip.*

The headnotes serve two purposes: first, to link Dreyer's writings with his film work, creating a double reflection through which experiential resonances may occur; and second, to bridge the gap between Dreyer's writings and readers who have difficulty identifying with him. As the Danish critic Ebbe Neergaard wrote about *Day of Wrath:*

Nothing is spoon-fed to the audience. You are asked to identify only if you can. But if you can you will be rewarded with one of the very rare experiences of the truth about human minds and hearts. How delicately and clearly it is all made . . . expressed only in little things, in sudden bursts of low-voiced singing in the quiet rooms with dark panels and the autumnal light seeping diagonally through narrow windows

. . . a touching yet tragically great drama about the simple, basic thing: the risk of being human.[2]

In that sense, this is, hopefully and intentionally, a book of risks.

After completing the writing and editing of the text to follow, I began working with a collection of photographs brought back from the Danish Film Museum in Copenhagen. I had a sense of wanting to select from this collection shots that illustrated the most essential points about Dreyer contained in his writings and my annotations and essays. I particularly wanted to provide graphic evidence against certain misconceptions about the man and his work, and to render visible some of its more elusive qualities. With the cooperation of my publisher, I was given latitude to expand this graphic dimension of the book. The presentation of these pictures now stands integral to the basic notion behind the format of the book: the double reflection of facing mirrors funneling images toward infinity. Perhaps through this the depth of field generated by Dreyer's films is at least suggested.

[2] *The Story of Danish Film,* The Danish Institute, Copenhagen, 1963, p. 78.

Swedish Film (1920)

Dreyer was just past thirty when he wrote this in *Dagbladet* (Copenhagen *Daily-Blade*). He had made only one film, *The President* (1920), and was preparing his second, *Leaves from Satan's Book* (1921). However, the piece is remarkable for the compression of personal film philosophy that it contains. Dreyer's sense of destiny for the new medium permeates each passage. He speaks about fulfilling a long-cherished wish to study in depth "the meaning of the Swedish art film for a Danish audience," and is aware of international influences upon the creation and reception of motion pictures. This sense of destiny carries over to the very personal and becomes, unfortunately, prophetic as Dreyer points a finger at the financiers whom, even this early on in the life of film (and in Dreyer's career), he discerned as having "never felt a sense of responsibility or mission" toward the evolution of film.

Two other motifs are introduced by Dreyer-the-critic that Dreyer-the-film-artist would continue to develop throughout his lifetime: the difference between "manufacturing" films and creating them with love and painstaking care. Dreyer would antagonize producers by taking all the time that was necessary for a film. He would also enrage them by building entire sets, down to the finest details, which, in themselves, might not appear on screen—except through the performances of his actors who were absorbing the environments he had constructed. The latter occurred most dramatically for *Joan of Arc* (1928), for which Dreyer had been given a blank check following the success of *Master of the House* (1925). He was never given such a blank check again. But as he matured he moved more toward selective distillation of objects and decor, something he called "abstraction," through which he reduced the elements of a set or location to a few penetrating essentials. The farmhouse in *Ordet* (1955) is a prime example of this and shows how this approach created an atmosphere somewhere between the very realistic, on the one hand, and the abstract, on the other. This was one of his most special qualities and something that audiences tend not to discern readily on the first viewing of his films. It is also the second of the motifs alluded to above: the search for the soul of a situation as opposed to standardized manners of *realism.*

A new Swedish film—*The Cloister in Sendomir*—has had its first performance, and that provides the occasion for the fulfillment of a long-cherished wish to study in depth the meaning of the Swedish art film for a Danish audience; but this can be done only by seeing it in its relation to the Danish and the American film.

The sad lot of the Danish film has been always to ride to death those subjects that throughout the world had been abandoned long ago. None of those who have had something to say has had the courage to take up the cudgels for something new, which again is related to the fact that leading film people here at home, in connection with their positions, have never felt a sense of responsibility or mission.

On the road that traces the evolution of film, there is no landmark that reminds us that *here* the Danish culture film cut new paths. If a memorial were to be erected, it would have to be in memory of the days when sparkling white wine was daily fare among film people and being well-dressed was the actor's only law. That was a golden time! But alas! not all that glitters is gold. The slightest scratch betrayed a very impure metal.

It was the time of the "Count and Countess" films.

The era was also remarkable because of the numerous new film factories that shot up like mushrooms from the ground. Yes, precisely: Factories! For in Denmark films have always been *manufactured.* It created a positive sensation when a man appeared—

Benjamin Christensen—who did not manufacture his films but worked them out with care and affection for every little detail. He was considered a little out of line. As things turned out though, it's clear that he was the one in contact with the future.

The flood of bad films that came out of Danish film factories during this period drowned the chances that Danish film had had. Favorable circumstances had created a world market for Danish film, capital existed in abundance, the only thing missing was that a man with the authority that taste and culture give should raise film to a higher sphere. But he did not turn up. A doubtful odor still hung over Danish film and frightened away the intelligentsia— an odor so persistent that the public in our more fastidious neighboring countries still hold their noses at the sight of a poster for a Danish film.

These words are not too harsh, for if the Danish film is ever to hope to keep up with others in the world film race, it is an indispensable condition that it see where it stands clearly and face up to things as they are.

But also for the sake of those who—without having followed film's evolution in recent years—continue to look down on it, also for their sake the truth should be told. When one wants to convert others, it is befitting to start by confessing to one's own faults, and it is wise to make concessions on points where others are right. And those who maintain that Danish films, taken as a whole, have never appealed to an audience other than the one that subscribes to *Leisure Time* and *Nick Carter*—well, they are unfortunately right, you know.

The best of the American films brought three essential boons: close-up photography, individual types, and realism.

The technique of breaking into a picture in order to show an important action in close-up has always been known about, but nobody dared to use it for fear of creating a commotion. The Americans taught us to use close-ups in a way that produced variety rather than disturbance. It is not difficult to show the importance of this little reform. In the long-shot the actor had to make use of gesticulations and large facial expressions. The close-up,

THE ARTICULATED CROWD. The gallery of faces: the jury in *The President* (1920), Dreyer's first feature. This photograph, and all following photographs but the last one, courtesy Danish Film Museum, Copenhagen.

THE ARTICULATED CROWD. Faces of the gallery: from Dreyer's film, *Mikaël* (1924), based on the novel by Herman Bang.

THE ARTICULATED CROWD. In the Jewish ghetto of *Die Gezeichneten* (Love One Another, 1922).

which betrays even the smallest twitch, forced the actors to act honestly and naturally. The days of the grimace were over. Film had found its way to human representation.

This reform has a certain inner relation to the Americans' conscious efforts in the direction of giving their films the *stamp of reality,* and to obtain this no sacrifice was too great. The greatest care was exercised to make each of the film's smallest details believable. But they went even further. With a keen eye, they picked for each role precisely the type of person that corresponded to the conception of the character, regardless of whether the part was big or small. Bit parts have often fixed themselves forever in one's mind. Who does not remember, for example, the gendarme in *The Birth of a Nation?*

With all these qualities, one might think that the American film was perfect, and yet—! Wasn't it as if something was missing? All of it was so real and so correct and so believable, and yet one did not believe it. One was always made interested, often impressed, but seldom moved. A devil whispered in one's ear: "Is it not all technique?"

—It was *soul* that was lacking!

It is not possible to mention Swedish film without mentioning Victor Sjöstrom's name in the same breath. He is the father of the Swedish *art* film.

At a time when "Count and Countess" films in this country were in fullest bloom, Sjöstrom broke away from the public highway and tackled two projects that were, for that time, quite inconceivable: *Terje Vigen* and *Bjerg Ejvind.* The keen minds of film, whose heads always shake in rhythm when something new happens, declared in unison that this was truly sheer madness. But Sjöstrom had set his course and steered it true regardless of the warnings that sounded around him. In all areas he had the courage to go against the current. He was perhaps the first in Scandinavia to realize that one cannot *manufacture* films if they are to have at least some cultural value. A nuance of language even today reflects two opposite views on this point. In Swedish the expression is "act out a film," in Danish it's "shoot a film." In Denmark, the focus of the work lies in the whirring photo apparatus, in Sweden it lies *in front of* the lens, *in the playing,* whose art becomes fixed on the celluloid stripping.

But Sjöstrom understood as well that the much-coveted film excitement could be obtained without using revolvers, jumps from the fifth floor, and similar sensationalisms. He understood that genuine excitement exists in all good dramatic material and he began to search among the most outstanding works of literature.—He also searched out his actors according to a completely new principle. In Danish practice there existed a ridiculous formula according to which all actors and actresses were divided into two groups depending on whether their looks were suitable for film or not. Talent and ability weren't part of the question. Sjöstrom cast exclusively on the basis of type and talent and the best names were not too good for him. In short, Sjöstrom applied to film the same rules and conditions that hold true in all real art.

For people who deal with art daily in its different forms of expression, it may sound strange to stress these—to them—common matters as being developments of a revolutionary kind. But we must not forget that we are dealing with a developing individual— an individual who has had to make his observations and gain his experience by himself, to whom, therefore, every phenomenon is both new and untested.

Through Sjöstrom's work, film was let into art's promised land, nor was he betrayed in his belief that strong literature should prevail over the screen novel, good dramatic acting over the puppet show, feeling over technique. Swedish film has gained world fame, and a flock of Sweden's best artists now rally under Sjöstrom's banner as directors, names like Gunnar Klintberg, John Brunius, Ivan Hedquist. And, besides these, Maurice Stiller, known as director of *The Blood-red Flower* and *Mr. Arne's Money,* an outstanding artist who, within Sjöstrom's broadly defined limits, has created an entirely personal form.

The Swedish art film has absorbed all the good qualities of the American film and left the bad habits behind, and it has acquired its distinctive character by becoming a medium for true and genuine human representation. The figures that populate the best Swedish films seem so alive that one almost feels their pulsebeats.—

And so these films bear the stamp of being imperishables. Just as good books can be read by generation after generation, for whom the yellowed pages and ornate language only give the enjoyment added charm, so will the best among Swedish films preserve through time their interest as valuable cultural documents.

On the ladder that signifies the evolution of film as a factor of culture, the Swedish film has placed the latest rung. More steps will be added—who will place them is still impossible to predict. But one thing can be said for certain: Sweden has for the time being every chance of keeping, for a long time to come, the leading position it has won with such shining arms.

There are still many who look upon film grudgingly, but it is precisely through the merits of the Swedish film that they grow fewer in number with each day that passes, and only in this way has film the prospect of gradually gaining full citizenship in the community of arts.

New Ideas About the Film:
Benjamin Christensen and His Ideas (1922)

This article appeared on New Year's Day, 1922, in *Politiken*. Benjamin Christensen was one of the pioneer individualists of the Danish film. The piece was occasioned by Dreyer's anticipation of Christensen's just-completed film, *The Witch*.[1] Dreyer rejoices that Christensen, who had shown evidence of true directorial sensibility in two earlier, rather lightweight films, had apparently finally made the kind of movie he'd wanted to make for many years.

An interesting feature of the article is its allusion to the idea of a *complete film poet or author.* Praising Christensen in advance of the film's release, Dreyer applauds his courage in choosing a subject of some cultural-historic significance. Dreyer quotes from Christensen's own remarks concerning authorship. Christensen is impatient with retold tales and proposes that filmmakers write their own scripts, reflecting the concerns of their own personalities rather than the personality of a writer whose work is being borrowed for the film. Dreyer agrees with Christensen's plea for originality, but then disagrees on the matter of the filmmaker himself writing his own scripts. Dreyer is rather insistent that the film director's task is essentially *interpretative* and best performed while working on the writings of someone else. But at the same time Dreyer sees the value of original material, the script written specifically for the screen: *the original screenplay.* His suggestion for resolution of this question is interestingly presented in the article itself. During his career, however, Dreyer never did realize production of an original screenplay. All of his major works were adaptations from theatre or literature. And in the one instance of an "original screenplay" that preoccupied his

---

[1] Known in the United States as *Witchcraft Through the Ages.*

later years—the completed scenario for a film about Jesus—
Dreyer wrote the script on his own.

It is certainly tempting to write about Benjamin Christensen, for
he, more than any other film person in Scandinavia, is an idealist
who goes to his work with holy seriousness. But it is by no means
easy, for the material that is available for a judgment of him as an
artist is very sparse.

As for his two earlier films, Benjamin Christensen himself would
probably be the first to protest against having them used as a yardstick for his artistic ability now. Certainly they meant a tremendous
step forward at the time, but what was surprising then was a working technique, dazzling in details, against which the manuscripts
seemed pretty mediocre. Times have changed. It is recognized on
all sides today that the manuscript is the fundamental condition for
a good film, and it is certain that *The Mysterious X* and *The Night
of Revenge* would appear quite faded if they were taken out again.

But behind these two films one caught a glimpse of the outlines
of a personality that is not common within the ranks of film people
—or at least was not common then: a man who knew exactly what
he wanted and pursued his goal with unyielding stubbornness
without letting himself become discouraged by obstacles of any
kind. It created a stir that he took half a year to make a film (usually eight to ten days was the norm). People shrugged him off as
a madman. The way things have turned out it is clear that he was
the one in touch with the future.

With the film that he has completed this fall, he should (if the
rumor is true) have broken his own record since over two years
are said to have been spent on the production. This is not quite
true though. One year out of that time was spent rebuilding the
studio in Hellerup, installation of heating pipes, etc. The shooting
itself has, strictly speaking, spread over seven months and of the

one and one-half million kroner the film is said to have cost, the rebuilding itself swallowed about half of it I daresay.

Much time and much money have been sacrificed on experiments of a technical kind and there is no doubt that *The Witch* will bring surprising news to the technical field. Thus, it has been said that Benjamin Christensen has managed to combine long-shots and close-ups in a way that simultaneously illustrates cause and effect. These technical steps forward are of great importance, for the more perfect film becomes in its technique the better it will be in a position to solve precisely that group of problems that the nonillusory theatre-stage must ignore. But the experts will know how to appreciate this pioneer work more than the general public will. The main thing for the public is the value of the thoughts that have been made to come alive on screen . . . the content of the film: *the manuscript.*

It has long been an open secret that *The Witch* is based upon the medieval witch persecutions and from there draws parallels between the famous sexual excesses in the convents of that time—and modern female hysteria. On the other hand, it is not known whether the film is formed as a popular scientific lecture, or if the material is treated poetically. If the first is the case, then Benjamin Christensen once again appears to be the pioneer who has the courage to bring a subject of cultural history to film *for the sake of the subject,* and since the problem is probably solved with imagination, there is every reason to look forward to this experiment with more than usual expectation. If he succeeds (i.e., if it pays off), the imitators will swarm. Innumerable other subjects of historic and cultural-historic kind (to take the most adjacent) will present themselves. Film will have acquired new land.

Maybe Benjamin Christensen has given the material of his film the form of a short story, and then the significance of the film itself will be measured by its ability to entertain, for no matter how sophisticated the direction might be, the mass audience's instincts will never be dazzled by the strange and new milieu unless the purely human story interests and moves them. It is another matter if the film, in addition to showing rare directorial ingenuity, reveals Benjamin Christensen as the *film author* or *poet* the world is waiting for; then he can be sure of world fame—or the martyr's halo.

In a local paper, Benjamin Christensen recently stated a number of reflections, which in film circles have been discussed animatedly man to man and all around. His view went something like this:

Film artists around the world seem, so far, principally to see their task as the retelling of old novels. There should be an end to this. The director must write his own manuscripts. The film artist (i.e., the director) must in the future, like every other artist, show us *his own personality in his own work.*

Benjamin Christensen is right in the first part of this: Screen versions of novels are a transitional stage that we must pass through as quickly as possible. But he is definitely wrong in the second part of his statement, for the task of film is and will remain the same as that of theatre: *to interpret other people's thoughts,* and the director's task is to submit to the writer whose cause he is serving. If the director is a personality, we'll certainly catch sight of him behind his work. Both Griffith and Reinhardt are examples of this.

Instead of isolating itself, film, on the contrary, needs to make contact with stimulating minds outside its own circle, and led by its own sound instincts film has, on its own, gone to the source of all art representing the human being: to *the poets.* So far, one has essentially confined oneself to the filming of nationally or—better still—internationally famous novels. What was said from the screen was only a repetition of already-known sentences. This situation will be changed only when film grabs the author's thoughts before they reach the publishing house management. *Those writers who in any way have the qualifications for it, must be brought to write directly for film,* and this is not at all as difficult as many who have become irritated with the idea of a "film manuscript" believe. The horrible monsters that in the old days were called "film manuscripts" do not exist anymore. *In the main,* the modern film manuscript has the form of the novel or short story, freed from redundant diffusion and with the episodes of the story closely gathered around the main dramatic line. In the description of the individual scenes, the author has complete freedom. For clarity's sake, I should like to mention an example from literature and I choose J. P. Jacobsen because he cannot in any case be accused of being influenced by the film. Anyone who is accustomed to seeing good films will be able to see that the scene quoted below, which is taken from *Mrs. Marie Grubbe,* both in content and mood can be transferred to film exactly according to the words and meaning of the book:

One night candles were being made in the servants' hall of Tjele. Marie stood at the copper mold, which was sunken down in a hay-filled vat, and immersed the wicks that the scullery girl, Ane Trinderup, Søren's niece, let drip off into a yellow earthenware dish. The cook took the platters, picked them up and hung them under the candle table, and took away the candles when they had become thick enough. At the servants' hall table, Søren Ladefoged sat looking on; he was dressed in a red cloth cap that was decorated with gold braids and black feathers; a silver pitcher stood in front of him with mead, and he was eating from a big piece of roast that he sliced with his clasp knife on a small pewter plate. He ate with great sedateness, drank from the mug, and responded now and then to Marie's smiling nod with a slow, appreciative movement of his head.

She asked him if he was seated comfortably.

More or less so.

So it was best that Ane go into the maid's room and get a pillow for him.

So she then did this, but not without making quite a few signs to the other girl behind Marie's back.

Wouldn't Søren like a piece of cake?

Yes, that wouldn't be so bad.

Marie took a wick spindle and went for the cake but stayed away rather long.

She was barely outside the door when both girls started to roar with laughter just as if previously arranged.

Søren frowned angrily at them.

I have with this quotation attempted to establish that for the author who wants to write directly for film there is no question at all of his shaping his material according to stereotypes and inartistic rules that are new and distasteful to him. Film does not want him to compromise with his artistic conscience. It wants him exactly the way he is, with all his individual peculiarities of style and form. Environmental description, painting a mood, detailed psychological accounting are not only permissible—they are a condition. What is required, after all, is only that the author *in the preparation of his material* show reasonable consideration for the needs of the film. From this, in turn, it follows that his "film novel" can be published in book form, which will be an artistic satisfaction to him and not without economic importance.

French Film (1926)

These comments on the French cinema, which appeared on May 1, 1926, in the magazine supplement of *Politiken,* are especially valuable for revealing the humor and humanity of Dreyer, who has been too frequently viewed at a distance as a "dour Dane." In the midst of pomp and ceremony, he longs for Chaplin. He pleads for films that are fresh, with open air and space, like the American Western, as opposed to the early French films, which always seemed to be canned theatre of one variety or another. And, at the same time, he cautions against technique for its own sake and the desire to impress the audience rather than to *move* it. All of these concerns remained with him throughout his life, and his films are replete with gentle humor, wit, and lack of pretension with rare, if not unique, consistency.

Some weeks ago at building number 14 Boulevard des Capucines, with a display of great and formal ceremony, a memorial plate was unveiled with an inscription reminding us that here, thirty years ago, the first film presentation took place with the device invented by Louis and Auguste Lumière. Besides the president and the mayor, the event was attended by a crowd of gentlemen in silk hats representing film's *societies* and *syndicates.* It was an extremely distinguished affair—I, for my part, just stood wishing that Chaplin would suddenly show up, in costume . . .

After the brothers Lumière put rockers on film's cradle, a time came when French film was the leading film of the world. It was built on traditions from the *Théâtre Français,* and everything was just fine until the Americans, with their sense of reality, found their way to the true nature of film. In contrast with the prairie films with their lasso-twirlers and wild horse rides, the French film, staged and shot from the wings, seemed dusty and artificial; it fell into discredit and the war killed it completely.

In recent years, however, it has started to revive. And for fear of the dust from the wings, things have gone to the other extreme: often French film is purely and simply photographic art—art in the sense of elaboration. One has experimented with the photographic lens in a thousand ways—placed prisms in front of it so that the picture was distorted, made it displaceable in order to make the picture "swim." One has put the device on wheels and on a turntable so that the picture slid or rotated, respectively, before the audience's unfortunate eyes. But all this hocus-pocus, too, now seems to be a thing of the past; they have realized that in the long run it won't do to give the audience stones for bread—and they are working toward giving expression to human moods and emotions.

It is not only in practice, though, that one works with film; it is scrutinized in theory, too. The well-known film idealist, theatre-manager Jean Tedesco, who is evidence that one can be a practical film man and an idealist as well, places his theatre, "Vieux Colombier" (known for its fine repertoire), at the disposal of lecturers. It is the beginning of a film academy. Through lectures by well-known writers, critics, and philosophers who have an interest in this new art, the seventh art is analyzed in all directions, while experts elucidate the artistic, technical, and commercial conditions and terms of the film.

They are really working with great energy to raise French film to its former heights—and since these efforts grow out of enthusiasm, I believe that they will succeed. It is not in France now the way it was in Germany some years ago. There, too, the industry was lifted up by a tremendous wave of energy, but the motive power was only the desire to impress, the hope of overpowering. But none of the films of that time, which were accompanied by enormous publicity noise, remained as monuments. For this they were too brutal

FUN AND GAMES. The young Walter Slezak, unstrung among the puppets, in the title role of *Mikaël,* with Nora Gregor.

FUN AND GAMES. Slezak, the Lady . . . and a certain tramp. *Mikaël.*

FUN AND GAMES. Through the loom, lightly: Mathilde Nielsen and Einar Rød in a moment of mistaken intention and identity from *The Parson's Widow* (1920).

FUN AND GAMES. Einar Rød as the phantom of many protuberances betrayed by his slippers (out of frame). *The Parson's Widow*.

FUN AND GAMES. The banquet scene in *Gertrud* (1964): homage to the great erotic poet.

FUN AND GAMES. The great erotic poet. *Gertrud.*

—devoid of heart and emotion. And *Variety,* which lately experienced such great success, is—despite the success—not the type of film by which German film will win.

Among the works people are expecting something from in this country are *Carmen,* which is directed by Jacques Feyder (the master of *Crainquebille*) and *Napoléon,* whose director is Abel Gance, indisputably the leader within French film. *Napoléon* will not only be the biggest film that France has ever produced but probably the biggest film in the world, since the gigantic work in itself comprises eight full films built on the most important periods in Napoleon's life from his youth to St. Helena. It is not possible to establish how many millions of crowns the film will cost, but it is known to be two or three years away from completion. It is the *Société générale des films,* of which Charles Pathé is president, that is financing this gigantic film, together, however, with some nationally minded rich men who contribute money without desiring profits in return (an example worthy of imitation by well-to-do Danish men).

I really wanted to see Abel Gance working, and press attaché Helge Wamberg, for whose helpfulness there is simply no measure, gained access for cartoonist Adolf Hallman and myself to Gance's studio in Billancourt. I did not regret it. I have been told that French studios are technically far behind—the truth is that Gance's studio, at least, is technically way ahead of the best ones in Berlin and probably equal to America's.

Altogether, I attended three shootings—all three times, mass scenes in which five to eight hundred extras took part. The first day, Gance shot a scene from the Cordelier's Club in June, 1792, where Napoleon for the first time hears the "Marseillaise" by Rouget de Lisle. The scene is very effective but gives, however, no real idea of Gance's outstanding talent. Perhaps he was indisposed; he was recently injured in an explosion and is still carrying his arm in a sling.

But at a second shooting some weeks later Gance displays all his virtuosity as a technician and organizer. It is a scene from one of Napoleon's battles that is to be shot. The whole studio is transformed into a wild and desolate woodland scene. An undulating terrain is made from stone and soil, giant spruces have been hauled in from the forest, in the foreground a little marsh is framed by live rush. Some officers are having a conference on a hill—on a hill directly across from them, Gance and his photographers have set up camp. Like big, strange insects the devices are standing in a cluster. At the center, Gance is sitting on a campstool and in a low voice is giving his orders as a host of assistants hasten to carry them out. He himself looks like a Napoleon as he sits there in all his calmness. Finally everything is ready and Gance signals that the action can begin. The arrangement is thought out so carefully in advance that a single test is enough. The scene is very effective. Powerful wind machines create "storm" and with their noise make the horses rear; from a pipe—and turbine plant in the ceiling—the rain is gushing down soaking the officers right to their skin in a matter of seconds.

For the third shooting, the scenery was changed. A hill was to be stormed and taken. "Dead" soldiers and "dead" horses are covering the battlefield where the fight is to take place. Just as in the second shooting, Gance turns up with an arrangement so carefully planned that the "battle" can be filmed without rehearsal. There are at least eight hundred men in combat; officers are charging up the hills on horseback at full speed. Banners are waving, a general falls off his horse, cannons from a distant fort spew out their fire over the battlefield—and in the middle of this turmoil the expert sees a soldier with a hidden camera. The camera is connected by an invisible cable to a motor outside the "battlefield"—it functions without a handcrank. Over the entire set, rain is pouring down, the wind machines send the gunsmoke howling across the undulating, fighting human mass, lightning is flashing—the effect is overwhelming.

When I, confused and shaken, leave the studio, I see the "wounded" gathered in the front room. The "warriors" have been carried away by the heat of battle to such an extent that they have received long slashes, scratches, and deep wounds. Blood is flowing. Two nurses go around dressing wounds, in one of the director's rooms a physician receives those most seriously injured. Gance himself probably doesn't give them a thought. I remember once reading a publicity folder for the Griffith film *Intolerance*. After reeling off how many millions of dollars had been spent, how many kilometers deep the sets were, how many hundred thousands of meters [of film] had been used, and how many tens of thousands of extras had taken part, it stated quite dryly in the end: During the shooting no human life has been wasted.

Only after having experienced the hospital scene described above, does this sentence take on any depth of perspective for me.

Realized Mysticism (1929)

This short statement, written at the time of the first release of *The Passion of Joan of Arc,* contains references to a number of pure "Dreyerisms." Falconetti played Joan for Dreyer by day and in the evening returned to her more usual performances in light, boulevard comedy. But depriving her of makeup, providing her with the full environment of the trial settings, and then developing her characterization rigorously and systematically resulted in one of the most memorable of all screen experiences. It is important to begin to qualify the popular impression of Dreyer as a mystic with the very canny, down-to-earth ways in which he went about representing the events giving rise to this reputation. Dreyer's unique achievement is poetic rationalization of the religious experience without detracting from its vitality or grandeur or reducing it to a scientific formula. Without recognition of Dreyer's own awareness of the special nature of "realized mysticism," the viewer may fall back on stock assumptions bearing in only the most general way upon the themes and issues Dreyer is treating. This is the specific problem many audiences have with the last five great films by Dreyer, especially *Ordet,* in which a heroine is brought back to life in broad daylight before our very eyes.

The virgin of Orleans and those matters that surrounded her death began to interest me when the shepherd girl's canonization in 1920[1] once again drew the attention of the public-at-large to the events and actions involving her—and not only in France. In ad-

[1] Dreyer gives this date incorrectly as 1924.—Ed.

IN THE MIDST OF LIFE. From *Mikaël*.

IN THE MIDST OF LIFE. From *Gertrud*.

dition to Bernard Shaw's ironical play, Anatole France's learned thesis aroused great interest, too. The more familiar I became with the historical material, the more anxious I became to attempt to re-create the most important periods of the virgin's life in the form of a film.

Even beforehand, I was aware that this project made specific demands. Handling the theme on the level of a costume film would probably have permitted a portrayal of the cultural epoch of the fifteenth century, but would have merely resulted in a comparison with other epochs. What counted was getting the spectator absorbed in the past; the means were multifarious and new.

A thorough study of the documents from the rehabilitation process was necessary; I did not study the clothes of the time, and things like that. The year of the event seemed as inessential to me as its distance from the present. I wanted to interpret a hymn to the triumph of the soul over life. What streams out to the possibly moved spectator in strange close-ups is not accidentally chosen. All these pictures express the character of the person they show and the spirit of that time. In order to give the truth, I dispensed with "beautification." My actors were not allowed to touch makeup and powder puffs. I also broke with the traditions of constructing a set. Right from the beginning of shooting, I let the scene architects build all the sets and make all the other preparations, and from the first to the last scene everything was shot in the right order. Rudolf Mate, who manned the camera, understood the demands of psychological drama in the close-ups and he gave me what I wanted, my feeling and my thought: realized mysticism.

But in Falconetti, who plays Joan, I found what I might, with very bold expression, allow myself to call "the martyr's reincarnation."

The Real Talking Film (1933)

As it develops its essential points, this article almost seems to be contradicting the position on "original screenplays" taken by Dreyer in the Benjamin Christensen piece. But, as with so much else in Dreyer, one must look closely and carefully and never make the stock assumption. What Dreyer is cautioning against, regarding material written directly for the screen, is lack of refinement and distillation. It is significant that he broaches the subject in an article on "the real talking film." In fact, unless one penetrates through to the subtext of what he is saying throughout the piece, it may seem a bit odd that he becomes involved in matters like "Jewish players for Jewish roles," or the addition of new scenes for screen adaptations of stage plays, and even the use of makeup. Each of these Dreyer presents as growing out of the possibilities that the coming of sound effected, but in a much deeper way Dreyer is reflecting on the sensitivity of cinema as a medium recording both sights and sounds. "Shadings," both visual and aural, were Dreyer's great preoccupation. This was nowhere more in evidence than in his very first sound film, *Vampyr* (1933), made the same year this article was written. At a time when many directors grabbed at sound for narrative-dialogic purposes, Dreyer immediately saw the *gestural* values of nuanced sound.

Finally, it becomes clear that Dreyer's opening passages calling for the film to "go back to the streets" are not a rallying cry for the replacement of the fiction film or the film of abstraction by the newsreel—again, a position apparently contradicting earlier and later statements by him. Rather, it is a call to filmmakers of all kinds to avoid studio moorings imposed by the arrival of sound.[1]

[1] See *A Little on Film Style,* written ten years later. Comparison of these two articles shows the development of Dreyer's struggle with and resolution of the problem of sound.

The ultimate importance of the Clemenceau footage, to Dreyer, is its demonstration of a technique applicable to many modes of film production.

This article appeared in *Politiken's* magazine (November 19, 1933).

I became enthusiastic about the talking film in 1928, when I saw and heard a film showing Clemenceau in his garden, a skullcap on his head and his cane in hand, the one that later, in keeping with his wish, was placed along with him in his coffin. Clemenceau, apparently, had not noticed the microphone but, irritated by the photographer's improvised questions—intended to make him "say something"—the tiger twisted and growled. The effect was grand. In a flash, that day, I saw how the real talking film should be— and my opinion has lasted till today.

Film started on streets and in alleys—as news reporting. Unfortunately, it was taken over by the theatre people, from whose embrace serious film luckily is slowly in the process of disengaging itself, for, in order to become independent art, film must find its way back to the street, to reporting. The real talking film must give the impression that a film photographer, equipped with camera and microphone, has sneaked unseen into one of the homes in the town just as some kind of a drama is taking place within the family. Hidden under his cloak of invisibility, he snaps up the most important scenes of the drama and disappears as silently as he came.

By this, the position of film to that of theatre is actually defined. A theatre performance is a picture seen at a distance. In order to make the general effect lifelike, one must paint with a coarse brush—the color must be laid on in rich blots. All details must be coarsened and enlarged—exaggerated. In the theatre everything is artificial and the whole idea is to bring artificial details into harmony with each other so that they produce a colored illusion of reality, while film represents reality itself in a strict black-and-white stylization.

The distance between theatre and film is given with the distance between *pretending* and *being.*

The manuscript is of fundamental importance to a film. It is certain that film, in order to renew itself, must go to the writers, but it is just as certain that a roughly prepared outline—an original, written directly for the film—is less valuable than a novel or a play where the material is prepared thoroughly and the thoughts have taken a final form. Since I define the real sound film as a film capable of fascinating by its psychological content, its story, and its remarks alone, without help from exaggerated sound effects, musical accompaniment, and inserted musical numbers, the psychological play is probably to be considered the most suitable material, on the condition, though, that the idea of the drama, its *raw material,* is extricated from the form of the play and transformed into film. That is to say that with consideration for the writer's intentions, his stage play must be liberated from all footlights-and-wings traditional dust and moved from the theatre out into life.

Characteristic of all good film is a certain rhythm-bound restlessness, which is created partly through the actors' movements in the pictures and partly through a more or less rapid interchange of the pictures themselves. A live, mobile camera, which even in close-ups adjusts flexibly and follows the persons so that the background is constantly shifted (just as for the eye, when we follow a person with our eyes), is important for the first type of restlessness. As for the interchange of images, it is important when the manuscript is adapted from the play that the play provide as much "offstage" as "onstage" action. This creates opportunities for new rhythm-making elements. Example: the third act of Kaj Munk's *The Word* takes place in the drawing room of the Borgen family's farm. Through the conversation of those present, we learn that the young woman who is to give birth has become ill suddenly and put in bed and that the doctor who has arrived in haste fears for her life and the baby's life. Later, we learn first of the baby's death and after that of her death. If *The Word* were to be filmed,[1] all these scenes in the sickroom, which the theatre audience gets to know only through conversation, would have to be included in the film. The actors going to and from the sickbed would contribute to creating the two types of restlessness or excitement that condition the rhythm of the film to an essential degree.

This addition of many new scenes demands a very strong compression of the dialogue, but it is amazing how one can keep on stripping a dialogue of entire speeches, sentences, words—without any other effect than that the writer's thoughts stand out even more clearly. *The talking film presents itself like a theatre piece in concentrated form.* For this reason, it is important that the poetic idea appear with the greatest possible clarity, even if it must be done at the expense of one nuance or another, for while the spectator in a theatre always has time and place to "recollect," i.e., to compare the remarks that are being said with previously mentioned information, the film is flickering away so quickly on the screen that the audience cannot possibly manage to pay attention to lines that don't have present value, i.e., are not absolutely connected with the situation that exists at the moment. Besides, there is often a possibility of *visualizing* parts of the dialogue, and here the close-up picture, which registers the smallest changes of expression, comes in very handy.

Finally, in producing the manuscript, one should aim at a unity of time and place, with the purpose of gathering all the bound-up tension of the material around the central idea.

The real talking film must not be photographed theatre.

One of the bad habits actors brought with them from the theatre to the film studio was the use of makeup. Not too many years ago, movie actors still wore wigs and beards but this, however, is becoming less and less common. Even the makeup is getting more discreet, and it happens that one sees completely unpainted faces in films, which seems refreshing, but it won't really be good until one arrives at representing all faces the way they are in life. The

[1] Kaj Munk's stage play *The Word* (*Ordet*) was first adapted to the screen by the Swedish director, Gustav Molander, in 1943. Dreyer released his own film version in 1955.—Ed.

new road that portrait photography has taken in the last five years has awakened a sense of the beauty of the natural, unpainted face. In film it is already inconceivable, even today, to let an old man be played by a young actor, and if I were to adapt Henri Nathansen's *Inside the Walls* to film, I would claim the right to cast all the people in Levin's house with Jewish players—actors or nonactors —for on film one cannot *act* Jewish, one must *be* a Jew.

Also, regarding the sets, film must one day understand its need to break away from the theatre. That they still, to this very day, for an ordinary modern movie build views of streets, house facades, and villa gardens in the studio, although the town is full of streets, houses, and gardens, is such a presumptuous thought that I don't even want to spend my indignation on it. Film must go back to the street—yes, more than that, it must go inside *houses,* inside *homes.*

When silent film passed away, techniques of illumination and optics were so far advanced that one would have dared venture the step—but then came the sound systems, which threw film back behind the sound-insulated celotex walls of the studios—and it will probably be long before it gets out from there again. Instead of shooting a film in constructed sets in a studio, one must arrive at shooting it in actually lived-in rooms. Against this, the sound technicians will object that it is impossible because of incidental, intruding sounds, but if one is striving to create a realistic room atmosphere, one must do the same thing as far as the sound atmosphere is concerned. While I am writing these lines, I can hear church bells ring in the distance; now I perceive the buzzing of the elevator; the distant, very-far-away clang of a streetcar, the clock of city hall, a door slamming. All these sounds would exist, too, if the walls in my room, instead of seeing a man working, were witnessing a moving, dramatic scene as background to which these sounds might even take on symbolic value—is it then right to leave them out? I believe not, but I reserve my final judgment until I have made a one hundred percent sound film in a studio.

On still another very important point one must free oneself from the traditions of the theatre, namely those concerning diction and the way of acting. The stage actor must calculate, when reciting his lines, that his words have to reach across ramp and orchestra pit all the way up to the audience in the balcony and in the gallery. This demands special handling of the voice and of diction. In the movie theatre, on the other hand, the spectator has the feeling of being face to face with the performers. In the real sound film, the *real* diction, corresponding to the unpainted face in an actually lived-in room, means common everyday speech as it is spoken by ordinary people. A sound film made with nonactors would doubtless be instructive for a study of the concept of film diction.

Peer Gynt at the Palace Theatre (1936)

This appeared in *BT* (a Danish newspaper, *Berlingske Tidende*) on January 21, 1936. Brief as it is, it still reveals Dreyer's preoccupation with going beyond broad strokes and into the subtleties of a situation, particularly psychological nuance. Nor will Dreyer accept unsuitable casting. He knows that the camera and screen will not let you get away with it and that the audience should not be expected to willingly "write-off" such lapses in selectivity.

The Germans have made a film of Henrik Ibsen's brilliant poem.

How was it?

As I was sitting in the Palace Theatre last night, an Offenbach refrain came to my mind, namely this one:

"I hear the sounds of boots, boots, boots . . ."

With sadness one felt the sounds of all the boots that have waded and stamped, plodded and clumped, around on Ibsen's work until all the psychological subtleties were trampled under and every little poetic flower was broken.

Where was Ibsen's Peer Gynt—that Peer who is no good at taking action and who therefore escapes into his dreams . . . the daydreamer who loves to give his imagination free rein, and who lies and invents without knowing where the one begins and the other ends?

Hans Albers, a man at least half-a-century old, could obviously not create a perfect illusion in the juvenile scenes, no more than Marieluise Claudius possessed the pure charm without which Solveig is not Solveig.

There is no reason to spend more lines on a review of this movie, which had only the period of time and fragments of Grieg's melodies in common with Ibsen's immortal work.

Boots, boots, boots . . .

The Gulliver Movie (1936)

Writing in *BT* on March 19, 1936, Dreyer took a long, hard look at Alexander Ptuschko's animated-doll film version of Swift's classic satire.

The idea of Dreyer as propagandist of the spiritual life, odd as the very concept might seem, is one that frequently appears in the attitude of many filmgoers. Dreyer's reaction to the Ptuschko film registers his abhorrence for any ulterior motive that would distract the filmmaker from his primary commitment to the work of art itself. Dreyer is so sharply aware of the issues involved in Ptuschko's distortion of Swift's masterpiece that one can begin to see how inappropriate it is to confuse his attraction to religious themes—as in *Joan of Arc, Day of Wrath,* and *Ordet,* particularly —as a vehicle for any institutionalized belief. This overriding humanism operates in *Gertrud,* as well, which attempts something much broader than *épater le bourgeois.* Dreyer was involved with *essences* rather than *issues.* Note how his mind works even in analyzing the nature of the appeal of the animated dolls. While technique draws his comment, his essential concern is with the depth-psychological mechanism through which the audience is moved.

In order to give a just judgment of this very-much-discussed Russian film, form and contents ought to be treated separately.

Let us take the contents first.

In Russia everything is under state control: factories, agriculture—and *art.* Once in a while one hears of artists who incur the leaders' disapproval because of their irregular gait. The director of this film, Mr. Ptuschko, need not have such fear: It must be due to pure coquetry that he has expressed his hope of having created a film that people can enjoy without noticing that they are being stuffed with Soviet propaganda at the same time.

The movie is based on Jonathan Swift's famed and venomously green-galled satire of the English society of his time. He didn't spare anyone, neither high nor low. The Russians have again poured venom and gall on the fable, but the gall this time is more red than green.

In contrast with Swift's satire that was aimed at society as a whole, this film turns against the king, parliamentarism, and the bourgeoisie, and glorifies the workers, who alone are noble, while the others are represented as imbeciles or idlers and parasites. The workers stand as if carved by Meunier, while all the others could have been drawn by George Grosz.

Such a one-sided distortion is incompatible with the demand for objectivity that applies to all art. Mr. Ptuschko has thereby disqualified his own work at the outset, no matter how interesting it otherwise might be for different reasons.

And now to the form.

As an introduction, we see a number of illustrations of Russian scout life, which are individually charming. The Soviet boy, Petia, who is a sea scout, dreams that he, like Gulliver, arrives in the country of the Lilliputians, and with the dream begins that part of the movie that is made without actors but only with the use of dolls with movable limbs and changeable facial expressions. It has to be openly admitted that Mr. Ptuschko, with this process, has obtained new and absolutely amazing effects that point toward a completely new type of movie.

Why do these scenes have such a surprising and fascinating effect on the audience? I wonder if it isn't because every gesture or movement in a human being that makes us think of mechanical dolls is ludicrous in itself? And even more so the stronger we feel the invisible mechanism! The more perfect the mixture of human and doll is, the greater the comic effect.

This is the secret of Chaplin's comic effects. His movements, postures, and gestures are those of the mechanical doll—he is a human but a doll as well.

With the performers in the Gulliver movie, the case is just the reverse. They are mechanical dolls whose movements, postures, and gestures are made as human as possible, although caricatured. They are dolls but also humans, and therefore the sight of them tickles our funny bones.

It was a work of exceptional patience. Over two thousand dolls have "participated." All the "leading roles" had exchangeable heads. The king alone had two hundred fifty heads with different facial expressions.

Technically, the experiment has succeeded; artistically, it is beside the point, because the work was not approached with clean hands.

The Jannings Film (1936)

Again, in reacting to the opening of a new movie and then responding to a reader's letter (*BT,* March 24, 1936), Dreyer reveals a highly developed cinematic consciousness. In the first part of the two pieces growing out of Emil Jannings' new film, Dreyer makes reference to certain distinctions between radio and cinema. He also shows the sharpness of his bite when aroused, and it is clear that the Nazis had gotten under his skin even in 1936. But aside from the wit and barbs, it is in the second of the two pieces that he begins to speak specifically about new techniques intrinsic to film. He calls for acting performances that grow from within, implying that the sensitivity of the camera picks up the difference between "dissolved and undissolved egos." It is clear from speaking with actors who have worked with Dreyer that he more and more developed a *field* approach to their performances as opposed to the more tightly controlled direction he seems to have applied to actors earlier in his career, certainly up to and including Falconetti as Joan. Performers who worked with him in the later films—*Day of Wrath, Ordet,* and *Gertrud*—refer to how little explicit direction he gave them and yet how, after a while, he seemed to cast a spell over the entire production, so that even the smallest remark or gesture from him, at the absolutely *right* moment, had transformational effect.

When the present regime came to power in Germany, one of its first actions was to purify German film and German theatre of non-Aryan blood. When the purification was finished there was nothing but sawdust left. The movies that have been brought out since then have been without blood, without nerve, sacks of sawdust!

The Jannings film, which had its first performance yesterday at the Grand Theatre, was a sack of sawdust like all the others—a sack with a hole in the bottom through which the sawdust seeped out, drip, drip, until the sack itself was left behind shriveled and shrunk. The sawdust was the endless (and dull) conversations and the indifferent small-town chatting, vaguely bordering on a conflict, which leave us completely cold because their main character is an otherworldly weave of thoughts. If one is to characterize this movie with a single phrase, one can make the point only by calling it a radio play, for the pictures were so completely superfluous. In this two- to two-and-a-half-thousand meters long movie there were twenty to thirty meters at the most that were real film, namely, the ending of the film's last scene. All the rest was—sawdust.

Jannings playacted—a few times quite effectively—but my how he playacted!

Of course, it is out of the question to talk about real directing, because the director's task, with regard to the entire character of the manuscript, must have been to poke at the hole in the sack so that the sawdust would flow in an evenly running stream. It was one of German film's veterans, Carl Froelich, who poked.

Dreyer's Reply (in *BT*)—About Playacting:
On the Occasion of the Jannings Film (1936)

It is the depth of his insights into the potentialities of film and the extent to which he was prepared to go for realization of these that places Dreyer in a class almost by himself among even the greatest filmmakers. He strove with rigor and consistency not only to get beyond theatrical indicating of expression but also to find and reveal quintessential visual tonalities. He would work with his actors so that an actor's face would not "tell" what he was feeling or experiencing but actually bring to the surface shaping energies from the core of the player's being-in-performance. Working with Maria Falconetti in *The Passion of Joan of Arc,* Dreyer describes the approach he would follow and refine throughout his career:

> With Falconetti it often happened that, after having worked all afternoon, we hadn't succeeded in getting exactly what was required. We said to ourselves then: tomorrow we will begin again. And the next day, we would have the bad take from the day before projected, we would examine it, we would search, and we always ended by finding in that bad take some little fragments, some little light that rendered the exact expression, the tonality we had been looking for. It is from there that we would set out again, taking the best and abandoning the remainder. It is from there that we took off, in order to begin again . . . and succeed.[1]

The young Norwegian actor, Baard Owe, describes working with Dreyer in *Gertrud,* more than three decades later. But there is a major difference: Dreyer apparently became less and less *direct* in shaping his actors' performances:

> He would come up to you after a scene and say something to you, anything it seemed, as long as it had absolutely nothing to do with the film. He would talk to you a few moments and then go away and then we

[1] From Michael Delahaye's interview with Carl Dreyer, first published in *Cahiers du Cinéma,* No. 170 (September, 1965), and reprinted in *Cahiers du Cinéma in English,* No. 4 (1966), translated by Rose Kaplan.

would do the scene over again. You knew you were doing it differently and later when you saw the different "takes" you marveled at the changes you had made. But of course you had played the scene finally just as Dreyer wanted it. You ended up playing the whole movie just as he wanted you to, only it wasn't until much later that you stopped believing you had been doing it all on your own.[2]

All of this suggests the approach through which the actors in a Dreyer film, though frequently playing parts originated for the stage, are brought to a truly cinematic style of performance.

Dreyer, himself, was aware of the difficulty of defining the processes involved in arriving at this kind of performance. He continued to work on the problem both in his films and his theoretical writings. Years later, in the essay he deferentially called "A Little on Film Style," Dreyer brought his thoughts on acting to their most advanced point taking away nothing from his sense of mystery about the process, but acknowledging the need and propriety of saying a few things that might at least suggest where the thresholds of contact with "the mystery" are most perceptible.

A reader reproaches me in an otherwise extremely kind letter for not having done full justice to the great German actor in my review of the Jannings film (at the Grand Theatre).

I have nothing against stating the reasons for my point of view more closely.

Actors can, according to my experience, be divided into two categories: those who build up their parts from the *outside* and those who build them up from *within*.

The first ones shape the role almost like the sculptor who covers a wooden skeleton with clay until it has a human figure. He attaches great importance to details of makeup and costume and equips the figure with different "characteristic" small features and

---

[2] In an interview with the editor, 1970.

PRETENDING AND BEING. Maria Falconetti as Dreyer's Joan of Arc. *The Passion of Joan of Arc* (1928). Pretending?

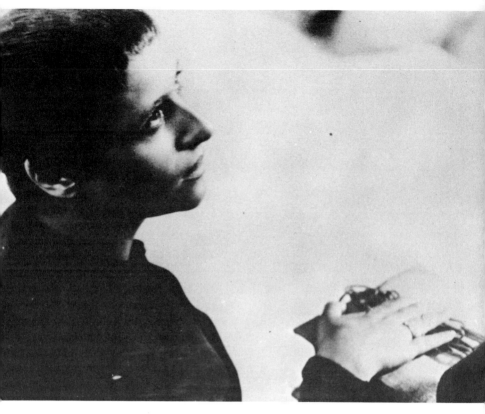

PRETENDING AND BEING. Falconetti as Joan. Being?

PRETENDING AND BEING. Antonin Artaud as Jean Massieu in *The Passion of Joan of Arc*. Outside—in?

PRETENDING AND BEING. Artaud as Jean Massieu. Inside—out?

gestures, e.g., a slightly stooping posture, a peculiar movement of the hands, a certain stroke with the glasses, a particular way of walking, a strange diction. Everything is deliberate, carefully considered and weighed, studied. When he has modeled in the clay long enough, the character stands as if "alive," and the skillful actor of this category makes sure that the many details are assembled into a whole. But the role's "ego" never becomes identical with the actor's "ego." Even in the most dramatic moments the personal "ego" stays outside, coolly contemplating, ready to correct if the physical "ego" falls out of the role.

This actor is *thinking* his role. He is *acting*.

The actor of the other category begins by identifying himself with the character he is to portray and he won't be satisfied until his heart is beating in the other chest. He *feels* the part, he *is* the other person and therefore he cannot avoid convincing us. All that is essential to the actor of the first category becomes of secondary importance to this one. He can act with his own bare face and we will believe him, because facial expressions, features, posture, walk, and gestures are determined *from within*. Example: Else Skouboe as Nora.

Jannings has always belonged to the first category of actors. When I think of the long series of big roles he has appeared in on film, I don't find a single deviation—except for some scenes in *Patriot X* where he, in some unforgettable moments, reached subtlety because he was suddenly carried away—*not* by the role but by what he himself felt. He forgot to think, and he let his feelings take over.

In the case of a talent and an intelligence such as Jannings', then, it is quite possible that his performance, which is built up from the outside, can approach the intuitive actor's art, which spontaneously arises from feeling and temperament; but there will always be a difference—the very difference between true and untrue, between real and unreal, between art and mimicry.

I cannot deviate from this perception, which is deep rooted, but so that the reader will not have written his letter in vain, I shall gladly admit that Jannings' playing in *Professor Traumulus* is perhaps his most accomplished and well-rounded performance to date.

Film and Criticism, I–III (1936)

In this exchange, printed in *BT* on three consecutive days, April 6–8, 1936, Dreyer articulated most directly his attitude toward the whole question of commercial compromise as faced by the film artist. He also defined the role and responsibility of the critic as he saw it. For Dreyer, each film that he made was an experiment, although after *The Passion of Joan of Arc* many critics feel that he moved away from daring formal innovation. Quite to the contrary, however, familiarization with the later films, from *Day of Wrath* to *Gertrud,* reveals the boldest experimentation with the most essential and most subtle elements of film. In his response to a lecture given by Dr. Schyberg and the exchange that followed, Dreyer, in plain words, makes it clear that he will never sell out to the spirit of utilitarianism gripping the commercial, box-office-oriented film industry. Dreyer opposes Schyberg's celebration of René Clair's emergence as a director of "usable films" by declaring that this later Clair *had* sold out and betrayed the earlier creator of masterworks like *Le Million* and *A Nous la Liberté.* Finally, and more than a little ironically, Dreyer repudiates the double standard of criticism—the scholarly, on the one hand, and the daily journalistic, on the other—implicit in Dr. Schyberg's argument. Here it is Dreyer, without benefit of academic degree, who calls for a single standard of artistic quality and integrity regardless of where a critic publishes his points of view. This unity of sensibility and intensity of commitment is consistent with Dreyer's own performance as a film artist throughout his life.

I: On the Occasion of Dr. Frederick Schyberg's Lecture at the Student Union

Unfortunately, I was prevented from being present at the Student Union's film evening at which Frederick Schyberg, Ph.D., expressed his views on film and criticism, which should not remain unchallenged.

To begin with, Dr. Schyberg points out that the chief purpose of all criticism is to invite independent judgment, so that the critic's task is to work *critically* by guiding the public according to personal points of view. That sounds reassuring, of course.

But one certainly gets worried when one makes closer acquaintance with Dr. Schyberg's "personal points of view," which are expressed summarily in the following remarks on René Clair:

> In the outstanding *A Nous la Liberté* René Clair experimented *toward* art but *away from* the public. In a later film, which was never shown in Denmark, he just about experimented himself completely out of the film industry and into unemployment. The joy one felt at his latest movie, *The Ghost Goes Along* [seen in the United States as *The Ghost Goes West*], could therefore almost be called a joy at the return of the prodigal director, a director regained for usable films.

If Dr. Schyberg had been a film producer, I could have understood his joy, but that he, *as a critic,* can rejoice is incomprehensible to me. For what is it, all things considered, that Dr. Schyberg rejoices at other than that René Clair has squandered his personality as an artist, for this is, as you know, the sad fact. Of the man who created *Le Million,* there is not very much left. Of course it is nice to know that René Clair escaped from being unemployed, but for film in general it would have been nicer if René Clair as an artist had remained the one he was. I cannot, like Dr. Schyberg, feel a little annoyed in seeing "the greatest cinematic talents make artistic conquests that later become beneficial to less brilliant directors." Indeed, I think it is splendid that there are conquerors and I think that it is precisely the task of criticism to encourage them to remain loyal to ideals and not stagnate—and at the same time force the producers to spend part of their profits from entertainment films on new artistic experiments. I wonder if it isn't an overall failing of the film that it has too few individualists—too few whole personalities.

Dr. Schyberg says, with a certain worry about Chaplin and René Clair (as he was), that they both represent "an art form by themselves . . . inimitable by all others." To call them "an art form by themselves" is, I suppose, only a paraphrase for individualists. But is it not a blessing that they are "inimitable," that they don't form a "rule" or a "school"? Wouldn't it be nice if there were many more "inimitable" personalities in film? I don't quite know what Dr. Schyberg thinks of this, for in another place he says: "Film is not one thing but many things," and in that he is right. At least it ought to be that way, but the truth is, you know, that the great majority of films give the impression of having passed through the same "assembly line." They lack the stamp of a whole personality; common to them is something strangely indistinct, blurred—originating from not having been created by one simple, strong personality but by an anonymous "organization," a kind of "kneading machine" for the manufacturing of what Dr. Schyberg calls *usable films*.

In connection with René Clair's "conversion," Dr. Schyberg emphasizes that, however unfortunate it is to have to demand audience appeal from a work of art, the demand is inevitable when it comes to films. But what is a film with "audience appeal"? Can Dr. Schyberg inform us about that? I don't think so, and it is just as well, for fortunately it does happen once in a while that a film that nobody "believes in" turns out to be a booming box-office success (e.g., *Nanook of the North* and *Maedchen in Uniform*), which will continue to stimulate artistically minded producers to new experiments. The new impulses came from that direction during the days of the silent film.

If the sound film wants to avoid stagnation, it must allow the renovators of cinema the same free play as in the days of the silent film, but unfortunately the tendency is going in the direction of sacrificing the personalities for the sake of leveling off at the ordinary.

To sum up, let me state that a critic ought to judge films from—

and *only* from—strictly artistic points of view without worrying about box-office matters or the director's worldly affairs. What the film wins or loses as art should be the only decisive consideration.

And as an ending, this: Dr. Schyberg extends me the honor of dedicating some observations to me by regretting that I have not succeeded, here in this country, in combining the artistic film with audience appeal. May I console him with the fact that I don't weep over my fate. I prefer to *have been* one of the conquerors rather than to be among the conquered at the price René Clair has paid.

II: Dr. Frederick Schyberg Answers Film Director Carl Th. Dreyer's Contribution to the Film Discussion at the Student Union

"Discussions" seldom result in anything else but disputes—and if people with *practical* knowledge of the things that are under discussion are really to disagree, it can, as a rule, only happen by ascribing to the adversary opinions that he does not have—and then attacking *them*. Now, the film evening at the Student Union was not, strictly speaking, planned as a discussion. The purpose of the evening was to *orientate* the members of the Student Union to the situation in film today, through three different lectures. In the discussion that followed, the floor was open to questions and counterquestions and differences of opinion, because the subject matter is now so much of current interest and so extensive that it seemed valuable to cover as much as possible in the course of the evening.

The subject of my lecture was "Critics," and what I had to work with, therefore, was not facts but *viewpoints*—or, more explicitly, viewpoints of the film criticism that is exercised daily, especially in the newspapers. From these viewpoints, Carl Th. Dreyer has gotten that I "wink" at the producers and the moneybags and that I am against the individuality of film artists, e.g., Chaplin and René Clair, among others. It is hardly possible to misunderstand me with more consistency. In my part of the lecture, I conducted a warm *defense* of Chaplin by pointing out the consequences of using a bigger yardstick as a basis for one's evaluation of a work of art than the one that lies in the work of art itself. Chaplin suffers today because, for a period of time, people wanted to make him "the film's greatest and only artist," while, in reality, he represents an art form in himself, connected to one particular person who cannot be imitated by others. I said something similar about René Clair, but not that he cannot be imitated but that he *should* not be imitated. Nobody admires the great, individual artistic personalities more than I do—but precisely for that reason, as a critic, I must wish that they be preserved for the art of filmmaking and not, after valuable artistic experimentation, lose the chance of being produced and hand over their possibilities (and their achievements of technical and artistic renewal) to the merely craftsmanlike directors.

Naturally, film's experiments must at any price *be supported* by the critics in the interest of artistic renewal. Who would think of claiming anything else or as a critic, in practice, fail in this respect? But I warned against the fashionable tendency, especially among young intellectuals, of raising experimental film to film in the proper sense of the word, to *the film* itself! The daily critics who work for the general public at large must not agree to this shifting in reasonable values, which raises experiments to *achievements* and fails to appreciate *practice* to the advantage of still-unclarified theory. And artistic experiments must win their victories not by "support" from the critics but by their own inner vitality, *their own ability to give rise to further practice themselves.* The director who, while still in his best years, has put himself outside the film industry has not—regardless of what meritorious achievements he can look back on from earlier times—attained results that the public, let alone the critics, can be satisfied with.

The comments about *"the price that René Clair has paid"* for his present activity—namely, that he "has squandered his personality as an artist," I gladly grant Carl Th. Dreyer. I know these expressions; in my ears they sound continuously meaningless. René Clair is an independent artist and as such *also* an experimenter. But the basis for his reputation lies in *his ability to communicate with the public through his art* (*Under the Roofs of Paris* and *The 14th of July*). He has renewed both himself and the film through his later experiments—but he has not *lost* himself in experiments or placed himself outside his profession. *The Ghost Goes Along* demonstrated this. It is the artist himself and through him the public that should benefit from the progress of art. All other experimentation belongs in the laboratory and to a narrow circle of experts—all that counts with the public is results. This viewpoint is not that of the scholarly film critic but of the journalistic, public film reviewer.

Carl Th. Dreyer, whose film direction I remember with admiration, has resented that I regret that he no longer makes films. He finds "consolation" in the fact that he doesn't weep over his fate. It is a shame that I must again offend him with my critical sympathy and interest. For the sake of art it is unimportant whether he "weeps" over his fate or not. But neither from an artistic nor a critical viewpoint is it unimportant whether the best abilities are utilized according to their merit or not.

III: Dreyer's Reply

To Dr. Schyberg's reply yesterday, I only wish to attach a few words.

I have lying in front of me in black and white that Dr. Schyberg, in his lecture, on the one hand, reproached René Clair for withdrawing from the public by being too much of an artist in one of his earlier films, and, on the other hand, expressed his joy that René Clair had now been regained by the *usable film*.

It was this comment that provided the basis for my contribution to the discussion and it is this comment that I will hold Dr. Schyberg to, for to me it is the heart of the matter under debate.

If daily newspaper critiques have any mission at all, it must be to act as the ever watchful conscience of art; and the critic, who not only tolerates but even approves of an artist who compromises with his individuality for the sake of popularity, commits a double treachery, in this case both against the film as an art and against criticism as a vocation. Every critic and every artist will agree with me about this.

Behind the Boulevards of Paris (1936)

Here in a piece from *BT,* May 12, 1936, is an example of Dreyer practicing what he has preached to Dr. Schyberg, turning the review of a routine film into a concise statement of a few essential film principles. Perhaps the most interesting thing about this review is the way it reveals Dreyer's keen awareness of the difference between approximation and accuracy, the whole matter of nuance and how the truth and reality of a presentation are achieved through sensitivity to proper shadings. And there is an especially revealing passage in which Dreyer comments on the difference between merely creating an illusion of a situation and making the audience experience it by feeling its many facets.

As a director, Bernard Deschamps does not have a great wing span. He neither plunges into the ravines of emotion nor rises to the peaks of poetry. He flies low and makes his observations and then, later, with infinite labor, applies them to the very thin, red thread that represents the story in his film. A niggling work, a thorough crowding of hundreds of details that please and bore us at the same time. A summing-up with modest results, because the combined quantities are all small. A film that pretends to be a slice of life but is not so because the director takes to sentimentality and melodrama.

The film divides into two parts, the second of which takes place ten to twelve years later than the first, which tends to weaken it dramatically.

In the first part, the narrative is shored up by a sort of irony which, in a pleasant way, strikes a balance between jest and seriousness. Here one is pleased by two lovely children, for whose sake alone the film is worth seeing, and Deschamps gets a chance to show his abilities as a portrayer of the Parisian petit-bourgeois milieu.

But with these abilities he fails in the second part of the film when the story changes into drama and demands human portraits. Here, Deschamps flatly gives up, becomes tiresome and banal.

The movie begins well and one is hoping for an experience—and is disappointed, for, apart from the children, and especially the boy, the movie does not offer anything new. Pierre Larquey is good as long as it is only a matter of creating an illusion, but he is not capable of making the audience share the feeling of loneliness that must seize him when the children leave him as grownups.

Poul Reumert has translated the film into Danish and composed the dubbed-in texts. Poul Reumert, undoubtedly, has a very good command of French but it is an old truth that in order to become a good translator it is more important to know the nuances in one's mother tongue than those in the foreign language. Reumert translates "Guignol" into "Marionette Theatre." I wonder if "Punch and Judy" wouldn't be even better? And why go round a direct translation of the slang word "marrant"? A Danish street urchin, in a similar situation, would say either "sjov" (funny) or "spy" (funny). The French "zut" is also considerably stronger than Reumert's "sa!" (oh, brother)—it must at least be translated into "sa for pokker" (damn it).

New Roads for the Danish Film—
H. C. Andersen (1939)

This essay, which appeared in the January, 1939, issue of the Danish periodical *Advertising,* is one of the most fascinating documents that Dreyer ever wrote. In it, Dreyer as a *comprehensive* man of cinema comes across very clearly and concretely. The ethereal, ivory-tower artist is nowhere to be found. In this sense, the article goes a long way toward dispelling the uninformed popular image of Dreyer as a man involved with and committed to his own narrow preoccupations with cinema. What the article shows, for all time, is how Dreyer encompassed the idealistic, the aesthetic, the metaphysical concerns about film and at the same time brought them into dynamic relationship with practical, businesslike matters necessary for the realization of visionary goals. Unfortunately, "business" was not as responsive.

The essay seems to fall into two separate parts, a first, in which Dreyer discusses the possibilities of a Hans Christian Andersen film biography, and a second, in which the discussion shifts to the question of a film version of one of Andersen's tales. But aside from the focus upon Andersen in each part of the article, there is an even more essential connection between the positions Dreyer takes on issues raised by each of these projects. Although three years have passed since his clash with Dr. Schyberg, Dreyer still sees the conflict between "business" films and artistic films as the central unresolved issue impeding the evolution of cinema itself. Each of his pleas reflects and is reflected in Dreyer's own work as a filmmaker. He calls for "plain, simple, and truthful" rendering of the life of the great Danish storyteller. One has only to recall the *mise-en-scène* of any Dreyer film to sense fully the spirit behind these words: the castle in *Joan of Arc,* the farmhouse in *Ordet,* and the special, informed directness of performance characteristic of actors in his films—these come first to mind. And he begs the Danish film industry itself to be *itself,* to show its own face in the making of such a film rather than take on the mannerisms of films made by other nations. If they're going to make a Hollywood film of Andersen's life, why not just let Hollywood make it in the first place (with Danny Kaye?).

Finally, he reaffirms his conviction that the camera captures more than "external resemblance," that its powerfully absorptive capabilities reveal "the missing incongruity" that we feel in a false or incompletely realized performance. It is the *congruity* of inner and outer energies that stamp the performances and productions Dreyer directed, a sense of deep contact between intention and execution absolutely organic to the central life of his films. This is what makes his change of subject in the second part of the article still deeply relative to the concerns of the earlier section. When he begins to discuss the question of a film version of an Andersen story, he immediately rules out the "merciless" photographic lens (opening on "live" situations) and proposes not merely an animated cartoon version but a movie "made by a Danish painter." He is specific about the distinction between what he has in mind and the "Snow White" kind of movie. The cartoon, to Dreyer, is essentially manneristic, limiting in a way not unlike the stock conventions of commercial films. What he sees is a liberation of the artist's individuality—something he fought for in terms of his own career all his life—expressing itself not in assembly-line cartoon panels drawn by an army of illustrators, but as a rich, individually stamped work "organically created from within." It is interesting to note that Dreyer refers to Oskar Fischinger as a pioneer in the experimental "drawn" film, achieving artistic goals far beyond those of the diversionary cartoon. His sharp awareness of Fischinger's preoccupations with purely graphic and plastic elements reflects Dreyer's own stylistic concerns cinematographically. Henning Bendtsen, his cameraman for *Ordet* and *Gertrud,* told me how Dreyer would arrange graphic elements within a scene (not to mention the lighting for which he was renowned) and then go to great lengths—once, breaking through an unused wall—to set the camera at exactly the right angle in relationship to setting and action.

It is agreed upon that Denmark is closer to the making of an H. C. Andersen film than any other country. It is also agreed upon that a sufficient amount of money and work must be contributed so that the movie becomes a worthy expression of our great national author and further propagates Danish culture and art.

It is a high and justified goal to undertake, and one must hope that those who have the courage to tackle this big task are also aware of both the difficulties and the responsibility.

The purpose of an H. C. Andersen movie sent out into the world in this way with the blessings of the Danish people must be to give a psychologically honest and truthful portrait of the author's life, as experienced by him and re-experienced in a re-creation that brings the audience into immediate closeness with the author as a human being and a personality. The description must be plain, simple, and truthful. No considerations other than the purely artistic and aesthetic ones should come into play.

Therefore, one must from the outset dissociate oneself from the thought of building the story of the film on an invented love affair between H. C. Andersen and Jenny Lind that has no basis in reality. As a reason and a defense for such a deviation from the facts it has been pleaded that first and foremost the film must emerge as a *movie,* i.e., a movie that people want to see. And, therefore, the film must have a *love plot,* for according to Hollywood, a movie without a *love plot* is worth nothing on the world market.

But since the film is to emerge as a worthy expression of our great national author, is it then quite worthy to take on such points of view? I wonder if an H. C. Andersen movie should not be thought of as a *sex appeal*-free movie? Anyway, one can name several movies that have managed quite well without a *love plot*— among others, the Pasteur film. And it is a misunderstanding to think that we enhance a film's foreign appeal by letting it emerge as an international factory product. On the contrary, it will win greater interest the more we show our own face and the less we grovel for foreign taste. We must avoid making a national film according to international taste. We must make a national film in accordance with our own ideals, a film whose only consideration is to raise a worthy memory of H. C. Andersen. There is only one of two viewpoints to take: either we must make the plain, simple, and truthful film about H. C. Andersen—or we must decide on a *business* film without sloppy consideration for the author's memory or national expectations. But if an H. C. Andersen movie is to be made from a Hollywood recipe, it is probably more sensible to leave it to the Americans after all. They can do it better in that case.

But if we decide to solve the problem in a psychologically and nationally defensible way, the people who put money in such a film should know beforehand that two conditions will assert themselves: first, that such a film will be very expensive because careful direction requires time, time, time, and time in film costs money, money, money; second, that extremely big expenses will be added if the film is to be sent out in more versions than the Danish, and without these versions with foreign actors the film cannot, of course, fulfill its purpose: to work abroad as cultural propaganda for Denmark. If one only intends to make two foreign versions (e.g., an English and a French one) besides the Danish one, the three hundred thousand crowns that from a certain side have been considered sufficient capital will actually constitute only a *fraction* of the whole sum necessary for the production of the Danish and the two foreign versions, and to a sober contemplator it must, from the outset, be regarded as entirely out of the question to interest foreign film capital.

There are other difficulties that should be kept in mind about the shooting of a biographical H. C. Andersen movie, and that is the performance of the main role. The problem is by no means solved just by engaging the most skillful actor for the role, of course. In film it is called "to be or not to be." It is not enough to have external resemblance; in addition, a resemblance in character, in psyche, in temperament, and in mentality are required. The photographic lens is ruthless. It forces its way right through disguise, makeup, and gestures. An effeminate character cannot, on film, be played by a masculine, strapping fellow, nor a sickly weakling by a healthy and robust man. The merciless lens will indeed betray the missing inner congruity, and we will feel the performance as a disharmony, as ingenuine. This is the reason that directors, for unusual roles, often prefer a type who has a character resemblance and thus only has to "be himself," rather than an actor who has to create the resemblance in character by external means. An H. C. Andersen biography on film stands or falls with the performance of the author's role, and a Danish actor who just approximately resembles the character doesn't exist for the moment.

A life portrait of H. C. Andersen will, as we have seen, collect a number of problems and difficulties, and one had better not underestimate them. Better to measure them than to ignore them.

But whatever happens or doesn't happen with the biographical H. C. Andersen film that the world waits and longs for, there is another H. C. Andersen film that sooner or later will be made and that we ought to start working on the sooner the better, the more so as its economical possibilities are far more favorable than those of the biographical film.

The thought has been advanced that no better characteristic of the author's personality can be given than by reproducing one or several of his fairy tales in pictures. This is true, of course, but not if one is imagining the fairy tales filmed, played, and photographed like an ordinary movie. The photographic lens is excellent for rendering palpable reality, but it is only a poor assistant when it comes to creating an illusion of the unreal, and faced with the cobweb-light fragrant poetry of the fairy tales, it will fail completely. In order to re-create the enchanting grace of the fairy tales on screen, film must turn to other means. *The real H. C. Andersen fairy tale film must be made by a Danish painter.*

When the first animated film came out many years ago, the more farsighted could predict that some day a "painted" movie, as opposed to the "acted" movie would emerge—a "live painting" corresponding to the "live drawing." The doubters from that time will hardly doubt any more, and, if they do, they should go in and see the Snow White movie.

One can often estimate how a movement is going to develop further by looking at its course up till now. If one takes a look back, it will be seen that, parallel to the purely entertaining cartoon films, certain artistic efforts have asserted themselves. Some of these efforts were of a purely abstract and experimental character. Here, one thinks especially of Fischinger, whose drawings usually showed only bundles of parallel lines which, to the accompaniment of some musical theme, moved rhythmically to the cadence of the sounds, now violently rising, now softly curving, now toward each other, now away from each other. It was a sort of music of lines.

One may think that these experiments were without interest to anyone but the professionals, but it is certain that the laws Fischinger could deduce from the rhythmical play of the lines, consciously or unconsciously, are expressed in every cartoon.

An experimenting Dutchman, Willem Bon, made some similar abstract experiments on the dynamics of color that undoubtedly have had significance for the color cartoon film.

Finally, there is reason to mention Lotte Reiniger, who some years ago produced a piece of absolutely delightful silhouette art in animated film—one of them, if I recall correctly, a single feature film on one of the Thousand and One Nights' fairy tales. It was an animated film with human figures and real action, and it was an attempt to renew the content possibilities of the genre as well.

We have seen the *entertaining* cartoon film unfold slowly under the influence of artistic stimulus from the outside until it has now blossomed most effectively into the Snow White film. One has the impression that the real *artistic* cartoon film is lying in wait somewhere just biding time until the appropriate moment to leap forth. This moment has come if we want it, and we have the possibility of guiding the leap in a direction favorable to us and deriving the first advantages from it ourselves.

We dare conclude without any further ado that the "drawn" film will develop into a "painted" film as the technique is perfected more and more, and will not confine itself to horror stories and fairy tales but tackle all the works that, because of their poetic or fantastic form and content, can no longer be handled with a camera, because the much-too-sober lens cannot, to a sufficient degree, replace the drawing or painting artist's brush and imagination. A number of important tasks thus await these artists, first and foremost the vivification of H. C. Andersen's fairy tales, and, in our neighboring countries, Asbjørnsen's fairy tales and Selma Lagerlöf's poetic narratives—for the Snow White film has already taught us that a cartoon is also capable of capturing a serious and solemn mood—I am thinking of the death scene, during which probably many people in the audience have shed a bashful tear.

After the fairy tales, the turn comes for more serious tasks: the edda poetry [eleventh-century Scandinavian poetry], descriptions of the saints, medieval lays—and, from literature, the fantastic tales by Edgar Allan Poe and E. T. A. Hoffmann. Maybe also Peer Gynt.

The cartoon will, from its present mannered style, step by step be lifted to an artistic level where the creative artist's individuality can unfold freely and his work emerge as a work of art, organically created from within.

This conquest for the artistic film should be greeted with joy, as surely as every endeavor away from the factory product toward the individually stamped work of art is always a good thing.

Besides, "painted" and "acted" film will exist side by side and thrive in sisterly understanding. They will share the literary material between themselves according to a line that separates poetry from reality, the supernatural, the fantastic, the lyrical from the naturalistic, the realistic, the prosaic. On both sides of this dividing line there will be a borderland in which both types of film will be able to hold their own almost to the same high degree. But let us go back to the Snow White film.

Measured by the yardstick of art it is not a prominent work, and—not mentioning its many enjoyable and charming qualities— one can point to imperfections, especially the somewhat picture-postcard psychology in the case of the main characters and also the often rattling and grating, often flat and insipid color effects. Walt

Disney is an entertaining and inventive cartoonist and very familiar with the craft of the cartoon, but he is certainly not a great artist.

Now it is obvious that the cartoon film, as far as style and literary content go, need not forever trudge in the footsteps of the weekly magazine's somewhat childish comic strips, and it is just as obvious that it lies within the limits of possibility to raise the animated illustrations of cartoon from its present form to a really artistic level. It is here, especially, that Denmark would be capable of making a contribution that could be of the greatest benefit to Danish art and Danish film.

We Danes possess in H. C. Andersen's fairy tales one of the greatest literary assets in the world. We also possess a number of important drawing and painting artists who have this advantage over all other illustrators and painters in the world, that they have sprung from the same soil and have absorbed the same atmosphere as H. C. Andersen. Should we not be the closest to the creation of animated H. C. Andersen fairy tale films, for which the Snow White film has paved the way?

To convince you, I ask you, in comparison with the Snow White film, to make the following supposition: Imagine a drawn or painted film of one of H. C. Andersen's fairy tales, made by Vilhelm Pedersen, or a drawn or painted film of one of Asbjørnsen's fairy tales created by the Norwegian fairy tale illustrator, Th. Kittelsen. There is certainly no one who will deny that each of these two has an imagination at his disposal whose exuberance is fully on a par with Walt Disney's, but their art is far more distinguished, more sophisticated, shows human warmth and sympathy behind the comic effect. Their drawings work like good music.

If today we were to think of producing a drawn or painted film of one of H. C. Andersen's fairy tales, the task, first of all, would be to find the Danish illustrator or painter now alive who, with the necessary technical aid, could "draw" or "paint" the chosen fairy tale best.

If it came to a competition, probably many more artists than one is inclined to think of in advance would solve the problem in a satisfactory way, for each Danish artist's spirit is in secret harmony with the spirit of H. C. Andersen's fairy tales. They would probably also turn out to possess the intellectual flexibility that would make it possible for them to adapt their form and skill to the needs of the cartoon film and thus, through their vivid drawings, speak to the avant-garde without losing contact with tradition.

Obviously, it is pure guesswork to mention names, but I think we can agree that Axel Nygaard's soft, graceful line and his colors filled with sweetness have all the qualifications for conjuring up the poetry in the lyrical fairy tales of H. C. Andersen. Also, Mogens Zieler's humor and grace justify the belief that he would be able to manage something so light and airy as *The Shepherdess and the Chimney Sweep, The Emperor's New Clothes,* or *The Princess and the Pea.* For the humorous fairy tales, like *Little Claus and Big Claus,* and *The Tinderbox* one dares suppose that Arne Ungermann, Hans Bendix, and Jensenius would be obvious. And for the dramatic fairy tales like *The Story About a Mother, The Traveling Companion,* and *The Wild Swans* there must certainly exist one or more painters among all of Denmark's painters, from Larsen Stevns to Hans Scherfig, who could preserve these fairy tales in animated film and make their special Danish character stand out as Fritz Syberg succeeded in doing in his illustrations for *The Story About a Mother.*

And once we start the fairy tales we will be surprised how many other tasks will become urgent. While on the subject, let me just mention Holger Drachmann's *Once Upon a Time—."* Imagine this wonderful Danish material, carried along by the most Danish of all Danish music, Lange-Muller's. Wouldn't this be a film with a message to the whole world?

It would seem inconceivable that no Danish film producer could be found who would let himself be tempted by this treasure chest that offers itself. The task is so obvious you could trip over it and far more simple to come to a decision about than a big, costly feature film. About fifty colored pasteboards would be sufficient in order to judge the suitability of the drawings to be transformed into film. Whether the interested producer then would try to realize the film in this country by summoning foreign technicians (if we don't already have ones good enough, which is what I am inclined to believe)—or should he prefer to ally himself with an English or American partner, is a secondary matter to begin with. The important thing is that there is a need for the "drawn" or "painted" H. C. Andersen fairy tale film and that Danish film should not wait until this rich national treasure is taken from our hands but rather should immediately set to work. The risk is little, for we know beforehand exactly what we are tackling and can follow the realization step by step. Furthermore, the experiences from the Snow White film have shown that a "drawn" film can be dubbed in other languages without any great difficulty.

The production costs for a technically irreproachable cartoon film in color and with sound will be about 60 crowns a meter in this country. Let us be *generous* and count on double for the fairy tale film. We will then see that a feature-length cartoon of 2,000 to 2,400 meters will cost *less* to produce than the Danish version alone of the acted H. C. Andersen biography. And while the cartoon film can be easily "translated" into other languages and consequently shown all over the world, the Danish version of the acted film can only be performed at home.

When the fairy tales have prepared the way, there may still be the desire for a biography, a gracefully drawn vivification of the most human of all H. C. Andersen fairy tales, namely, his own— "The Fairy Tale of My Life"—lovingly and charmingly braided into the story of the ugly duckling who became a beautiful swan. I can see this animation before me in a warm tone of red chalk, created by a great Danish artist. Denmark cannot give H. C. Andersen a finer and more beautiful memorial.

This kind of biography will offer, among other things, the advantage that, in characterizing the author, one can include all the highlights of his life, from the time when he was in the cradle until he was at the summit of glory. This would be impossible in an acted film, if only because no single actor would be capable of playing H. C. Andersen as a child, as a youth, as a man, and as a conference advisor. In a drawn film it will also be far easier for the gentle artist than for the performing actor to defend and present in a sympathetic and tolerant light H. C. Andersen's naïve and "odd" manner.

In this connection, it is worth recalling that there exists, for use in a proposed illustrated edition of "The Fairy Tale of My Life," a collection of colored illustrations from the hand of the painter Larsen Stevns that not long ago were exhibited at The Free [a gallery] and excited great admiration because of their dramatic style. These illustrations were not produced with the animated film in mind, I suppose, and thus cannot be judged as such, but they still might be able to give a hint.

Since the appearance of sound film, Danish film has not had any possibilities on the international market. Properly grasped and taken up, the thinking sketched above will give Danish film a chance of again creating a national film production on an international basis.

Film Technique and Scripts:
Some Comments for Kjeld Abell (1939)

Obviously someone had touched a Dreyer nerve! And in very clearly defining the boundaries of the director's terrain—as you shall read in a moment—Dreyer's response needs little additional dialogue. But the verve with which he performs this task of setting the record straight is worth noting. It is a vitality that lies at the heart of some of his most serious work as well, a wittiness that has apparently eluded many viewers but that is nonetheless present in his films. One need only recall the banquet scene in *Gertrud.*

One thing further: the particular "artistic intuition and immediate feeling for rhythmical balance" that Dreyer sees coming from the director and the director alone, from first draft to final cut, can be discerned in any one of a number of uncannily realized scenes from the films themselves. I mean scenes in which, without contorting or distorting the surface imagery in any noticeable way, Dreyer seems to manage to liberate inner energies so that they pour from the screen while still firmly contained within the natural elements of the surface action. There are many such instances in Dreyer's films but one that comes to mind especially with regard to this point occurs in *Day of Wrath,* when Anne—played by Lisbeth Movin—comes to Martin for the first time as a lover within the very house in which they live with his father, the man who has taken the much younger Anne as his wife following the death of Martin's mother. Miss Movin moves across the room toward Martin as if her whole life had been compressed into the single action. It is difficult to recall other cinematic moments in which such intensity has been realized through so simple means. It seems, indeed, to have come from the emergence of a deeply established rapport between script, director, and actor executed with just such "intuition and immediate feeling for rhythmical balance" as Dreyer refers to in this piece, which is from *BT,* January 26, 1939.

The gentlemen Kjeld Abell and Arne Weel have crossed swords in *Politiken* these last few days. The reason for the duel is a critique of Danish cinema made by the author Harry Søiberg. Without wanting to meddle in the conflict, I should like to point out an error that Kjeld Abell and no doubt many others along with him are guilty of. It is with regard to the script (the film manuscript, scanned in images, from which the director works in the studio).

"Who in this country can write a real shooting script?" Kjeld Abell asks, suggesting that authors must be closest to it and, as he believes, that a script should come into existence through a preceding collaboration between author and director.

To this I will reply that the shooting script itself ought to be worked out by the film director—*and by nobody else.* It is definitely the film director's job—*and his alone.* The screenplay can and should be made by the author and the director in collaboration, but the director alone should have responsibility for the (shooting) script. It is he who is the intermediary between script and screen. He has to visualize the writer's thoughts. It is he who has to "see" the images, not only "see" the individual images but "see" them in their changes and succession. It is he who creates the rhythm of the film through the selection and linking together of the motifs. The composition of the script is therefore the director's rightful work, in the very truest sense of the word, and if he doesn't resist with his hands and his feet other people who meddle in it, he lacks understanding of what the real tasks of direction consist in.

To let others work out a script for a director would correspond to giving a fully worked out drawing to a painter and asking him to put the colors on. Just as, for the artist's eye, lines and colors

COUNTRY MATTERS. From *The President.*

COUNTRY MATTERS. From *The President*.

COUNTRY MATTERS. From *The Bride of Glomdal* (1926): ". . . artistic intuition . . ."

COUNTRY MATTERS. From *The Bride of Glomdal:* ". . . and an immediate feeling for rhythmical balance of images."

constitute an indivisible whole, so too, for the film director, composing the picture and directing are inseparably connected. Therefore, a shooting script is not a "technical" but, in the highest degree, an "artistic" matter. Through the script the director proves if he is an artist or not. From which it again follows that the director's collaboration in the preparation of the manuscript is not only desirable but absolutely necessary. For only he, in his thoughts, is capable of carrying the lines of the manuscript further into the shooting script because he is the only one in whose mind the many elements a film consists of are fused into a unity.

It is not a question of "technique and technique over and over again"—as Kjeld Abell writes. It is an artistic intuition and an immediate feeling for rhythmical balance of images that is necessary when the manuscript is scanned in images—consequently something one has inside oneself (if one has it) and not a technique that can be learned. And therefore, a preceding collaboration between author and director will not lead to artistic results unless the director is an artist—more exactly expressed: a film artist.

In other respects, I fully agree with Kjeld Abell that film should not be photographed theatre but wholly and completely film. The innermost essence of film is a need for truth, and it lies in its nature to shun exaggeration and hollowness.

Two Plays That Flopped: Was It the Fault of the Direction?, and an Exchange of Letters (1939)

This was something other than a straight review of a play or two that Dreyer undertook in *BT* on April 4, 1939. The Danes were being menaced by their German neighbors; a year later they would be Occupied. Dreyer regrets, with quiet outrage and open frustration, that two plays embodying the values of the culture he defends failed to engage the audience and "flopped." He traces this failure with sensitivity and in detail, revealing the kind of consideration and analysis he brought to bear upon projects of his own. In responding to Mogens Dam's reply, Dreyer also shows —vis-à-vis his adversary's letter—the difference between the mind that follows things "to the letter" and the mind that is able to discern the inner spirit of instructional words. But then, at the same time, Dreyer proves how clearly and concretely he analyzes theatrical cause and effect in terms of moving an audience.

Dreyer's awareness of the special dynamics operating within the theatrical medium provided the base for his aesthetically successful transformations from stage to screen. He had full grasp of the distinctions among media—literary, theatrical, and cinematic. Because this understanding penetrated to essentials, he was able to build his cinematic effects with subtlety and sureness. If one recalls *Day of Wrath* and *Ordet* as Dreyer brought them to the screen, one becomes aware of cinematic transformations occurring not through the obvious "adaptational" modes but with the deep resonances characteristic of film used for its primary strengths. Dreyer did not merely "move things outside" gratuitously—because the camera "could go there." Rather, he carefully orchestrated kinetic, tonal, and compositional elements intrinsic to cinema. Comparing, for example, Dreyer's treatment of the nightmare-dream sequences in *Vampyr* with Ingmar Bergman's parallel scenes in *Wild Strawberries,* Michael Roemer wrote:

SURFACES OF (UN-)REALITY. Baron Nicolas de Gunzburg, alias Julian West, as David Gray (*Alan* Gray in the Aryan version shown in Germany) in *Vampyr* (1932).

SURFACES OF (UN-)REALITY. The Vampire and her doting doctor. Henriette Gerard as Marguerite Chopin, the Vampire, and Jan Hieronimko, the doctor.

SURFACES OF (UN-)REALITY. The impatient shadow. *Vampyr*.

Audiences can be 'played' by a skillful moviemaker with a fair amount of predictability, so that even discriminating audiences are easily taken in . . . The nightmare quality [in the *Wild Strawberries* dream sequence] is derivative. The deserted, shuttered street, the clock and watch without hands, the glass hearse, the faceless man are all conventions familiar to surrealist painting and literature. Bergman uses them skillfully and with conviction to produce an effect in the audience, but they are not true film images, derived from life and rendered in concrete, physical terms.

There is a similar nightmare in Dreyer's *Vampyr* . . . Here the detail is concrete: an experience is rendered, not cited: the situation is objective and out of it emerges, very powerfully, the feeling that Dreyer is after . . . Once again we note that the unassuming detail can render a complex feeling (or meaning) that eludes the more obviously ambitious but abstract statement.[1]

Was It the Fault of the Direction?

Karel Čapek's *The Mother* has played now for the last time at the Betty Nansen Theatre. Two important plays with world reputation have now flopped within the last few weeks. The first one was Robert E. Sherwood's equally remarkable piece, *The Great Madness [Idiot's Delight]*, at the People's Theatre. Both works are of simply frightening topicality and in a dreadful time, have a message for all of us.

If one wants to look for the reason that these two very interesting stage productions fell, one cannot ignore the fact that the theatres share greatly in the blame, too.

To mention *The Great Madness* first, there is, in my opinion, no doubt that it is the play's violent final effect, as presented by the People's Theatre, that is to blame for the cool reception the play received.

As is well known, the play ends with a bombing of the health

[1] "The Surfaces of Reality," *Film Quarterly,* Vol. XVIII, No. 1 (Fall, 1964).

spa that is the setting for the story—a bombing on the open stage: a single ear-splitting explosion, darkness and silence, suggesting total destruction—followed by a slow curtain fall.

The explosion came so unexpectedly and with such force at the People's Theatre that everyone had to think that the bomb had fallen on the theatre itself, and for some seconds the audience was seized by a genuine and palpable fear that loosened its grip only when the houselights came up.

Anyone who has studied this effect even for a single evening will have seen on the faces around him the forced smiles that expressed embarrassment and shyness. People were vexed that they had let themselves be taken by surprise. The fear reaction was relieved in a kind of resentment. One was not far from considering oneself the victim of an ugly joke. Just as the bomb's impact wiped out the image on stage, so, too, it wiped out the real feeling of fear that the spectators had endured, the rising emotion that they could not have avoided feeling, especially during the play's last two acts, thanks to Else Skouboe's and Erling Schroeder's marvelous acting.

The director had here sinned against an elementary dramatic rule. The stronger and more violent an effect is, the better it must be prepared for, so that it does not produce audience backlash. This all-annihilating bomb explosion should have been prepared for through perhaps six or seven detonations of increasing force, corresponding to bombs dropping from an approaching enemy plane, and accompanied by the more and more overexcited dialogue between Irene and Harry, suggesting that the next-to-last bomb has hit the electric power line: darkness on the stage—— the fear of death sets in upon the two——propeller noise of the plane directly overhead——and now the explosion in the hotel itself——a dying person's last, futile call——a sobbing——a word, one single one, the last. And then it's all over.

If the final episode had been arranged according to this or a similar plan, the increasingly violent excitement would have found its gradual release in a natural way. As it was, the ending tore the developing mood to pieces instead of completing the steeply rising line.

In the Betty Nansen Theatre's production of Čapek's moving drama, something similar occasionally manifested itself; but the greatest weakness lay, however, in another place. As great and gripping as Mrs. Betty Nansen's own performance as the mother was, just as great was the lady's misunderstanding in her staging of the dead who appeared before her.

With the years, the mother has become clairvoyant and sees her dead before her. But it is only she who *sees* them. There is no meaning in the rest of us *seeing* them. We are only to *sense* them, *feel* them as something unreal that glides through the room on-stage, shapeless and colorless forms, restless in their longing to return to the grave. The dead have no faces, their features are blurred. Because they have become accustomed to the darkness and solitude of the grave, they avoid light and approach only with reluctance only those living people with whom they have the past in common.

The flaw in Mrs. Nansen's dead was that they were not sufficiently dead.

As a rule, Mrs. Nansen placed her dead in footlights or even in the cone of light from a projector that had been installed "for the occasion." Only occasionally did they glide into the half-light, while it ought to have been just the reverse. Their voices ought to have sounded out to us from the half-light, their shapes should have been just dimly seen, only occasionally might they have grazed the light from a lamp. For just a few seconds toward the end of the second act it was like that, and the effect was overwhelming.

Mrs. Nansen's dead lacked the stamp of unreality, and therefore that special atmosphere intended by the author as background for the drama failed to appear, and many of the play's episodes became painful instead of having a releasing and liberating effect.

When it is a matter of such precarious stage phenomena as apparitions for an open curtain, one profits by being satisfied to give only suggestions and let the audience's imagination take care of the rest. It (the imagination) serves as at least a dozen stage technicians—therefore, theatre has never had so great a power over the mind as when there were still tallow candles and oil lamps for lighting.

But Mrs. Nansen left nothing or very little to the imagination. The dead were brought so close in on us that we could see what color socks they were wearing.

For a theatre that offers an artistic or cultural contribution, it is always satisfying to know that this contribution has been rendered completely. If the performance then flops, at least it falls with honor. But neither the People's Theatre nor Betty Nansen's Theatre can pride themselves for that. They did not render the full contribution, which is so much the more regrettable because we in a time like this cannot afford to lose any work that takes up the cudgels for the preservation of the culture and the ideas that we profess.

The Stage-Life of the Dead: Mogens Dam's Reply

Dear Mr. Carl Th. Dreyer!

In *BT* of April 4th you set yourself up as a judge about two performances about which *BT*'s excellent dramatic critic, Professor Hans Brix, has long ago expressed his opinion and—at least in the case of *The Mother*—in very enthusiastic terms at that. But that of course is between you and Hans Brix. It's another thing entirely that the hypothesis you set up regarding the reason that Čapek's play "flopped"—an assertion, incidentally, that stands on your say-so—is utterly wrong and should not remain unchallenged.

You write:

As great and gripping as Mrs. Betty Nansen's own performance as the mother was, just as great was the lady's misunderstanding in her staging of the dead who appeared before her.

With the years, the mother has become clairvoyant (I think you misunderstand the word *clairvoyant,* Mr. Dreyer!) and sees her dead before her. But it is only she who *sees* them. There is no meaning in the rest of us *seeing* them. We are only to *sense* them, *feel* them as something unreal that glides through the room onstage, shapeless and

colorless forms, restless in their longing to return to the grave. The
dead have no faces, their features are blurred. Because they have become accustomed to the darkness and solitude of the grave, they avoid
light and approach only with reluctance only those living people with
whom they have the past in common.

Here you are already in direct conflict with the author's own
words. The dead do not long for any grave nor do they approach
the living reluctantly. Čapek, who does not at all establish where
the dead *qua* dead reside, explicitly lets one of them mention that
the dead restlessly circle about the rooms and in the places of the
living and do everything to call the attention of those alive to their
presence. But, as we will see, it gets even worse! You write further:

The flaw in Mrs. Nansen's dead was that they were not sufficiently
dead.

As a rule, Mrs. Nansen placed her dead in footlights or even in the
cone of light from a projector that had been installed "for the occasion." Only occasionally did they glide into the half-light, while it
ought to have been just the reverse. Their voices ought to have sounded
out to us from the half-light, their shapes should have been just dimly
seen, only occasionally might they have grazed the light from a lamp.
[For just a few seconds toward the end of the second act it was like
that, and the effect was overwhelming —*Editor's note:* Mogens Dam
does not include this sentence in his reproduction of Dreyer's statement.]

Mrs. Nansen's dead lacked the stamp of unreality, and therefore,
that special atmosphere intended by the author as background for the
drama failed to appear, and many of the play's episodes became painful instead of having a releasing and liberating effect.

Apart from the fact that one shudders at the thought of how you
yourself supposedly—according to the staging you outlined—would
have presented us with light-shy, sneaking ghosts of the kind one
sees in manor houses and in amateur theatricals, with long white
sheets and green faces and bony hands—why not skeletons, too?—
may one be permitted to ask from where you so coolly pick up
the arrogant statement about "that special atmosphere intended by

SURFACES OF (UN-)REALITY. Jane Mora as the nurse in *Vampyr*.
Moving toward the darkness.

SURFACES OF (UN-)REALITY. *The President*. Groping toward the light.

the author as background for the drama"? You have presumably
discussed this with the deceased author or possibly read it in the
manuscript?

No, you have indeed not! For it so happens, strangely enough,
that the author in his preface to the manuscript expresses precisely
his opinion and his demands on this difficult point. *And it is directly contrary to yours!* Karel Čapek writes in the beginning of
the manuscript to *The Mother,* not as a stage direction in paren-
theses, but as a strongly underlined memorandum that he demands
be respected:

The author wishes to point out that the dead who are here in the
play moving around the mother must not be regarded or performed as
ghosts but as living, pleasant, and confident human figures who move
quite naturally in and out of the old home and gather around the light
of the lamp.

They are exactly as they were during their lifetime, for this is the
way they go on living in the mother's consciousness, only dead in the
sense that she can no longer hold them in her arms and that they make
less noise than living people.

May I draw your attention to the phrase ". . . go on living in the
mother's consciousness"; in my opinion, it says everything. No
wife and mother need be "clairvoyant" in order to continue to
live with her dead in this sense. The author has shown us this
without any false use of half-light or ghost-illumination.

Now you can, of course, declare yourself wiser than the author
if you dare to, but it doesn't shake the fact that Mrs. Nansen's
wise and moving production of *The Mother* hit right on the mark.

The reason that this beautiful and wise play was not seen by
nearly as many as should have seen it is difficult to reach an
agreement on. It is an unfortunate fact, which you and your
"ghosts" hardly could have improved upon.

(signed)
Mogens Dam

"When the Dead Live":
An Objective Reply to Mogens Dam

Dear Mogens Dam:

I am pleased that you should turn up in a discussion regarding the production of *The Mother* at the Betty Nansen Theatre. But it is not pleasing that you are not objective in your contribution. And you are anything but objective when you try to impute to me that I would want the dead played as "light-shy, sneaking ghosts, with long white sheets and green faces and bony hands." There is in what I wrote not the slightest basis for such an assumption. For what did I write? I reproached Mrs. Nansen for letting her dead bathe themselves in footlights and spotlights, only occasionally allowing them to glide into semidarkness. We saw live human beings before us, but we were asked to believe that they were dead. I maintained that it would have been better if the voices of the dead had sounded out to us from the half-light. Their figures should have been barely visible, only occasionally grazing the light from a lamp. That is precisely what I wrote. Nothing about the white sheets, green faces, bony hands that you—a little perfidiously —want to impute to me.

To talk objectively now, I am still of the opinion that Mrs. Nansen as a director should have been able to bring us to see the dead the way the mother saw them, i.e., the way we all see our dead, if we possess that faculty. The question is, then, how do we see our dead. If one dares at all engage in a definition of this, I wonder if we then do not see them the way they appear before us in our dreams—vague and receding and impalpable? I think so.

It is this conception that you find "utterly wrong," and as proof, you refer to a preface that the author has written in his manuscript. But unfortunately for you, "it so happens, strangely enough," that his conception precisely covers mine. He imagines the dead as they were during their lifetime—*however, they make less noise than living people.* In this last sentence lies clear indication of just this stamp of unreality that I missed so much. The writer does not want these dead people to press themselves forward on our senses. Therefore, the silence, like space laid down between them and us, creates distance, remoteness. But silence and darkness are twin sisters. Darkness deepens the silence, and complete silence implies complete darkness. Both darkness and silence have an inciting effect on the imagination. Therefore, as I see it, Mrs. Nansen would have acted wholly in the author's spirit if, to obtain *the unreal stillness demanded by him,* she had enveloped her dead in a subduing, dimming half-light, so that these dead would be presented as what they are: phenomena of the subconscious mind. We should see them as such. Subdued, projected out of the gray darkness of eternity. We should see them as when they lived—and yet differently. Nearby and yet far away.

In my opinion, Mrs. Nansen did not succeed in giving us the sensation of this unreal reality demanded by the author. Her dead were alive *and only alive* (with the exception of the pilot, who was very close to being right). In her staging of the dead, Mrs. Nansen paralyzed the audience's imaginative faculty instead of exciting it into collaboration, derailed the public's fantasy instead of sending it further out. Thus, the spectators were prevented from fully acquiring the author's work and went away unsatisfied, for the task of the stage image is to set the audience's imagination going, and no theatrical impression becomes an adventure of the spirit without the cooperation of the imagination.

Forgive me for saying so, but your (and Mrs. Nansen's) interpretation has more to do with literature than with theatre.

With kind regards,
Yours,

Carl Th. Dreyer

Photography in Danish Film (1940)

No one had more of a right or better qualifications to address himself to the subject of photography in the Danish film; and yet for reasons best known to himself—possibly very practical ones, possibly whimsical—Dreyer published this article under the pseudonym of "Filmman." It is hard to say whether the article began as a review of three recent Danish films that then brought forth from Dreyer this brief on camerawork, particularly lighting, or if Dreyer set out to discuss the general question of cinematography and got down to cases by reference to the three films cited. In either event, and quite characteristically, concision and incisiveness combine within the piece to transcend any occasionality and provide us with part of the answer to a major question: through which elements did Dreyer himself achieve the distinctive, intensely evocative camera and lighting effects found in all of his films?

It is clear from the first passages that the key to effective photography, as Dreyer saw it, depended upon the consciousness of the artist himself. Problem-solving is seen as the catalyst of inspiration, and "impressive effects" often grow out of humble need.

Also, we do well to note that Dreyer's comments are not merely of the compendium or checklist-of-helpful-hints sort. Rather, what he writes grows from an awareness of some quite elusive cinema dynamics, functions of graphic energy through which his own films achieve their unique qualities and effects. Certainly, Dreyer's references to "interplay of light and shadow" are best illustrated from films like *Day of Wrath, Ordet,* and *Gertrud,* as are his references to "supple use of the mobile camera," backgrounds that should be *felt* rather than *seen,* and the rhythms within a main rhythm that "the audience feels without being aware of how it comes into being." For each of these, one can recall a memorable instance from Dreyer's films: the muted chiaroscuro of *Vampyr,* for which the cameraman, Maté, used gauze over the lens for a number of exterior scenes; Bendtsen, the cameraman on *Ordet,* at first a bit puzzled at Dreyer's insistence upon continually small camera movements, not merely to adjust framing but to create almost unnoticeable rhythmic gestures within a relatively static setting.

Certainly, there is much of "the silent language" implicit in Dreyer's *mise-en-scène* concerns, as expressed in the article below, and also in the manner of relationship between director and cameraman. On the one hand, Dreyer's emphasis upon effects that the audience is moved toward almost subliminally—rather than signaled onto through conventionalized means—perhaps suggests the nature of the special problem of audience response to his films. The viewer must open himself to Dreyer—to the pace of action, the penetration of images—and then be secure enough within himself to respond spontaneously to screen energies that do not make obvious gestures of solicitation. Think of the quiet but tense opening moments of *Day of Wrath,* when Herlof's Marthe is hunted and terribly alone; the domestic scenes in *Ordet;* or almost any close-up of Nina Pens Rode as *Gertrud.*

And, on the other hand, Dreyer's good fortune with cameramen was hardly accidental. Henning Bendtsen, his cameraman on *Ordet* and *Gertrud,* describes the development of his artistic relationship with Dreyer as one that took place slowly, over a period of weeks of waiting for good weather in Jutland at the very start of the filming of *Ordet.* Deep rapport of more than just a technical kind grew between the two men, so that by the time filming really got underway an almost unspoken dialogue of intention and execution continually passed between them.

It's not only the food but the way it's served. In this regard (as in several others) Danish film can learn from American film, which makes even vitamin-deficient food go down by serving it on a silver plate.

But—one will object—Danish film cannot afford silver plates. This is not true. One is inclined to attribute a greater role to "the technique" than it is entitled to. What counts is the man behind the camera. Give a good photographer a camera worth eight kroner and he will make good pictures. Give a bad photographer a Leica or a Zeiss-Ikon and his pictures will still be bad. Give a mediocre cinematographer twelve thousand amperes (of light) and his footage will become worse rather than better from it, while the real craftsman in a pinch makes do with seventy amperes and still obtains impressive effects.

No, it is not "the technique" alone that does it. It is also the man. He has it in his power to create the atmosphere that leads us to believe in what is happening on the screen. He can support the director's intentions, he can also counteract them. If he has a real feeling for the interplay of light and shadow, he can, through his exposures, create a certain light rhythm that works together with the film's other rhythmic elements and thus contributes to the film's main rhythm—the one the audience feels without being aware of how it comes into being. Three Danish films have opened during these last weeks, and from this, one has had the opportunity to make comparisons and altogether form an impression of film photography in this country. In the film *Watch the Turn in Solby,* one is immediately pleased by the light and pleasant photography that is made to come alive through supple use of the mobile camera. There are many evocative images in this film, particularly a few of the night shots in the vicarage and midsummer-bonfire pictures from the lake. Unfortunately, the gentle summer-night atmosphere from these last ones has not been carried over to the inserted close-up pictures, which therefore interrupt the effect obtained instead of rounding it off. It also hurts one, in most of the outdoor shots, to see a gray-white and toneless sky without any form or design. Where are the clouds? They should have been elicited with a yellow filter. Some forest pictures (without sky) are absolutely delightful.

In the indoor pictures one notices an inclination to light up the background too much. One must not forget that the task of photography is, through the exposure, to draw the spectator's eyes

TONING AND ATONING WITH LIGHT. *The President.* Early tendency toward room simplification, but the overlapping, split shadows would
never have been allowed in later films.

TONING AND ATONING WITH LIGHT. *The President.* Artificial twilight of a demigod.

TONING AND ATONING WITH LIGHT. *Day of Wrath* (1943). Lisbeth Movin and Preben Lerdorff Rye. Rising.

TONING AND ATONING WITH LIGHT. *Day of Wrath*. Preben Lerdorff
Rye and Lisbeth Movin. Falling.

toward what is essential in every single shot—usually the acting—and a little high gloss from a too strongly exposed gilded picture frame is sufficient to distract the audience to the detriment of the actors. The background must only *be felt,* not *seen.* Incidentally, most often front light is used, which in many instances makes the faces whitewashed and unmodeled. There are, however, many successful close-ups.

To go right from this film to *The Child* is like coming from sunshine into overcast weather. The prevailing mood in *The Child* is gloomy and without warmth, and the cumulative impression of the photography is: accidental. One encounters nasty things in the course of the evening. In immediately successive close-ups of the same actor, taken from the same spot, the background is sometimes overexposed, sometimes pitch-black. In rooms with overhead lighting, the shadows are crawling up the walls; in rooms with table lighting, down the walls. Somewhere an actor throws a very distinct shadow on the wall to his right, although the dominating source of light in the shot is a table lamp, placed in front and to the left of the actor, therefore almost between him and the wall. In short, there are plenty of shadows. In another place, where an actor goes through a door, he is accompanied by *several* shadows. How many, I cannot say, for I did not have time to count them.

There are several good, clear shots in the film, neat and orderly work—but not a single one that burns itself into the memory. And it teems with false lighting. In semidark rooms, only lighted by a table lamp's weak glow, we see the people act with a flood of light streaming down on them like the strongest tropical sun. And Lis Smed's hair often shines so much that one would think it was on fire.

What one feels regarding the photography of this film is first and foremost the absence of an artistic will that sets up a goal for itself and consciously works toward it.

About the photographic work in the third film, *In the Good Old Days,* there would be many nice things to say if the film had been built around a naturalistic subject. There are many good images with fine, rhythmic lighting effects; I am thinking particularly about some pictures from the stable, but of others, too. The portraits are generally excellent, the figures gracefully modeled, and the character of the action set off in relief by the lighting. What one regrets, however, is that the camera has passed over an artistic task that imposes itself, namely, to have reminded the audience constantly, through a particular photographic style, that it is a dream, a fantasy they are witnessing, possibly through a conscious distortion that could have carried the action away from naturalism and into parody.

The conclusion of these observations is that Danish film has at its disposal clever and conscientious photographers and that they just need the courage to choose a particular style for each individual film that must then be carried out with will and logic from first image to last.

A Letter to *Politiken* (1943)

The letter that follows appeared in *Politiken,* January 5, 1943. It is a rather short statement but, for purposes of putting together the Dreyer mosaic, of tuning in on the Dreyer wavelength, this letter reveals a side or capacity of Dreyer that is frequently ignored or not discerned as part of his makeup and the makeup of his films: *Dreyer was not cut off from his anger.* Rather, he was capable of direct, spontaneous response when attacked or insulted. He was very much in contact with himself and had access to a complete range of emotions. Far from being monuments to piety, the films of his mature period rather glow and crackle with inner outrage. They are not "angry films" but, equally, they are not soft celebrations of the righteous. Untuned to this dimension, the viewer perhaps misses the way in which *Joan of Arc* is about *committees;* fails to feel the bite *at* false piety in *Day of Wrath;* and misses the allegorical subtext that *Vampyr* manages to sustain without losing its directness and immediacy.

On the occasion of Mrs. Betty Nansen's having declared that she has "thought about" attaching me to her film project as a "technical assistant"—I should like, with these lines, to inform the lady that she can save herself the trouble of asking. I cannot be engaged as a "technical assistant," but only as a director with *full artistic responsibility.* And as a director Mrs. Nansen probably will not want to engage me when she hears that not even in my dreams would it occur to me to let her play the Virgin Mary.

Besides, I am quite satisfied to be at Palladium Studios, where, hopefully, by the time Mrs. Nansen would begin her production, I myself will be in full swing with my first film for them, *Day of Wrath.*

Copenhagen
January 5, 1943

A Little on Film Style (1943)

The characteristic conviction about what he writes is deepened still further in this essay, which first appeared in *Politiken,* December 2, 1943. The Germans were occupying Denmark. Dreyer had recently completed *Day of Wrath,* his first feature film since *Vampyr* (1932). It was a movement of recapitulation and summary, the reflections of an artist who had perhaps wondered if he would ever have the chance to work again.

The essay is filled with Dreyer's consideration of a number of cinematic issues that had been brewing during his previous decade of artistic inactivity. Certainly Dreyer had not been inactive mentally, but aside from the short film on unwed mothers, made in 1942, it was only through *Day of Wrath* that his thinking about cinema had been put to a test and objectified for evaluation. Viewed this way, *Day of Wrath* can be seen as a transitional film between his evocative initial exploration of sound, *Vampyr,* and the emboldened experiments with image and dialogue relationships that occur in his last two films, *Ordet* and—especially—*Gertrud.* This consideration of sound, occurring in the central part of the essay, is a key to the style Dreyer was constantly working to refine. And his closing comments on acting are the most illuminating he was ever to publish. These elements, *sound* and *acting,* are his preoccupations in this essay, along with the question of camerawork and cinematography, which he could never avoid for very long.

Henning Bendtsen, the cameraman on *Ordet* and *Gertrud,* told me that Dreyer wanted expressive camera movements rather than mechanically utilitarian pans or tracking shots. He described how Dreyer would either ask for these directly or, after they had worked together for some time, approve of Bendtsen's introduction of such nuance. The "nuance" might be a sudden acceleration at a particular point in the movement of the camera or a slowing down or even stopping and fine readjustment. Bendtsen was awed by Dreyer's awareness of when a thing had been done just right and when it had missed even slightly. When Dreyer speaks of "a continuous, flowing, horizontally gliding movement" however, he is not referring to camera movement alone. Although such motion is included, his remarks refer to the effect of the whole *mise-en-scène,* the total compositional materialization of what is envisioned, as it occurs on screen.

In his films, Dreyer builds and controls a certain "taking-your-time" ambiance, and it is, of course, one of the things most held against him. But the slowness of his style is a very dynamic kind of impedance. Dreyer knew that the screen is two-dimensional, "flat" in itself, and yet he regularly spoke of the viewer's eyes resting on and in the image. This referred to the total absorption of visible material and also to the fuller entering into the drama, and here he played upon a third cinematic dimension: time—through which the experience became cumulative in an inward-going way. Do Dreyer's films bore or do they *bore into* the viewer? Are they merely slow or do they cultivate, by extending the image in time, visual *retards* that shift the experience to a more subjective, penetrative dynamic beyond accustomed intensity? Dreyer expresses keen awareness of the difference between the image that involves the viewer through flow or flight and the image that involves the viewer through *immersion.* In Dreyer's films, from *The Passion of Joan of Arc* on, but deepening with each succeeding work, we are asked and given the opportunity to shift gears from our habitual snap-crackle-and-pop narrative surfing and to go *into* the images, to absorb and be absorbed by the rich phenomena of the apparently simple individual scene. Because the flow of the action is deliberately impeded by the extended, relatively static scene (as opposed to the montage sequence), attention is permitted to accrue upon the sufficiency of information present in the given moment: the *presence* of the present is heightened. This contributes not only to the intensification of the experience offered —familiar or not—but allows our grasp of nuance, of implications and connotations, to refine our total perception of the scene: our sense of what is happening or of what simply *is* becomes more accurate. And, in Dreyer, as he himself indicates below in the passage on "the one right expression," accuracy is a way of arriving at a new level of consciousness.

The development of Dreyer's sound film style, particularly his use of dialogue, seems to contain a paradox that may be confusing and disorienting when understood only in part. The disorientation is crucial, because it tends to generate false expectations about what one is likely to experience in a Dreyer film, and the wrong expectations inevitably lead to misdirection of the perceptual set or attitude through which the film is received. Consequently, like a fielder breaking the wrong way for a ball, the chances of the viewer "catching"—Dreyer's own word—what the filmmaker has *sent* is greatly reduced.

The contradiction seems to occur in Dreyer's attitudes and practices regarding the balance between words and images. The conventional notion about Dreyer is that, as a great filmmaker, as a man of the cinema who had earned his credentials for all time with *The Passion of Joan of Arc* and *Vampyr* (to say nothing of the remarkably proficient earlier films), he would necessarily carry forward into the sound era—inviolably, giving no quarter, aid, or comfort to the enemy—sound-in-its-most-antipathetic-form: speech. However, with each film, from *Vampyr* to *Day of Wrath* to *Ordet* and finally *Gertrud,* the quantity of dialogue, ironically, increases. The first reaction to *Gertrud* among some critics and audiences was that Dreyer had virtually defected from cinema, had, because of health or age, taken the shortcut of dialogue to tell his "story" and forfeited all things truly cinematic.

Whether the viewer will ever warm to Dreyer's deepening film style is the viewer's own business. As Ebbe Neergaard observed, "You are asked to identify only if you can." But it helps not to assume straight off that the filmmaker, due to loss of power or failure of nerve, bumbled into bad results. It helps not to assume that the great man left us and himself behind. And with Dreyer the evidence is clear, both in the progression of developments within the films themselves and in his own carefully considered statements of intention. This 1943 essay captures rather beautifully Dreyer's struggle with the problem. It shows his mind in action. He does not seem to have resolved the question of a balance between words and images in all of its particulars as yet. Different ends of the problem keep coming up and at times seem almost contradictory. At one point he says: "Sound films have an inclination to push pictures to the side . . . (they talk) all too much, while the eyes are seldom given permission to rest on a good picture effect." He is impressed by the way "pictures . . . sink into the spectator's consciousness." He speaks of his own, just-completed film and how he worked for a quiet rhythm of players "feeling their way from one to another." He also refers to "fast rhythm," to "films where the pictures were whipped up to . . . rhythm for the sake of rhythm." He does this in response to complaints that his films are too slow. Natural enough! But then comes the crux of the matter: he attributes the whipped-up rhythm to the silent film, calls it an inheritance from that time to the era of sound. Suddenly, he seems to be saying that the tendency not to give images their due, not to let the eyes absorb effects—"to rest," as he puts it—results from two things: (1) too much talk, and (2) the silent film! Paradox? Let us see:

It becomes more evident that Dreyer, in this essay, was working toward an awareness that would become the basis of his stylistic development throughout the remainder of his filmmaking life. It isn't sound versus silence that is on Dreyer's mind, or even talk versus image. What Dreyer is most concerned about mastering is the penetrative power of his visuals, the depth to which material projected on screen can "sink into the spectator's consciousness." As he first began using sound, in *Vampyr* and then *Day of Wrath*, Dreyer approached cautiously. Even *Day of Wrath* has the earmarks of the fragments-of-dialogue mode used so directly in *Vampyr*. But with *Day of Wrath* the visual rhythm has already begun to slow down and move decisively away from the impactive montage of *Joan of Arc*, and, to a lesser but not less clear degree, *Vampyr*. With *Ordet*, the final balance is before us: the reduction of details through high selectivity in the *mise-en-scène*, what Dreyer frequently called "abstraction." *Ordet* is also marked by the slowing down, generally, and in a few scenes almost to the point of stasis, so predominant throughout *Gertrud.*

It is clear that Dreyer's tendency toward monumentality, toward the sculptural and the static, is a function or a means through which he achieves the penetrative force and accretion of consciousness that is his most essential stylistic quality. The paradox yields; one sees how this master of the silent film found his ultimate cinematic liberation *through* the elements of sound and speech. Through speech, Dreyer was able to provide the narrative impetus, the horizontal movement across a dramatic situation and its unfolding events. And he found that, properly handled, he did not have to gain this at a loss of "letting the eyes rest," which he felt the silent filmmaker had been forced to sacrifice and the early sound films had "pushed to the side." Dreyer's final stylistic resolution was achieved through near-separation of narrative and graphic functions of film—but in an oddly balanced way. The separation is mediated by imbuing dialogue with gestural as well as informational elements. In the last films, especially *Gertrud* (and the cause of all its troubles!), Dreyer intensified the degree to which each of these techniques was refined. A sense of gentle abstraction permeates the film. One cannot deny that the viewer must participate in the final synthesis. But why not? Understanding the dynamics of Dreyer's slowing things down, matching the acuteness of his selectivity with equally discerning reception of the *mise-en-scène,* is part of the agreement: as long as "[his] pictures were worth seeing and [his] words worth hearing." And Dreyer has seen to this.

It has been observed that no "school" has sprung up around Dreyer, no disciples noticeably working in the image of the master. Perhaps it is because Dreyer leaves no handles protruding from what he does. He has spoken and written about a tendency toward abstraction that works out in practice as a refinement to essentials. This abstraction needn't be the more eye-catching upheavals of visual syntax of a *Last Year at Marienbad* (1961): they can occur, for Dreyer, through other components of a movie—

pace and rhythm, for example, or the lighting—wherever primal energy from the core of the work is brought to form at the surface. Style is not imposed upon the situation but rather grows from it organically. This sense of the organic, of the energy of a scene generated from the film's center rather than grafted on or cleverly imposed is Dreyer's way with film (and something he was able to articulate as early as the 1936 article on the acting style of Emil Jannings). And when Dreyer speaks of a style that "saturates and penetrates," he means this literally. He is calling attention to a basic property of film as film: the photosensitive substance that runs behind the lens of a camera. Elementary but crucial!—particularly to Dreyer with his awareness of the absorptive capacity of the stuff, how it will soak up and record phenomena to which it is exposed. Dreyer realizes this potential to an incredible degree, but in deceptively simple and direct ways. Not only will film soak up the large objects in view—the Proper Nouns of a situation—but it will bring to light normally elusive details and nuances and gather them together into a field. Generating this field, polarizing all of the elements within it—the actors, first of all—is Dreyer's overriding objective. Only in this way can he see the paradox of a collective art resolved into a unity, the potentialities of film—"my only great passion," as he called it—realized to a worthwhile degree.

There is a certain resemblance between a work of art and a person. Just as one can talk about a person's soul, one can also talk about the work of art's soul, its personality.

The soul is shown through the style, which is the artist's way of giving expression to his perception of the material. The style is important in attaching inspiration to artistic form. Through the style, the artist molds the many details that make it whole. Through style, he gets others to see the material through his eyes.

Style is not something that can be separated from the finished work of art. It saturates and penetrates it, and yet is invisible and undemonstrable.

All art is a single person's work. But a film is created by a collectivity and a collectivity cannot create art unless an artistic personality stands behind it and acts as its driving force.

The first creating impulse for a film comes from the writer whose work is the actual foundation for the film. But from the moment the poetic foundation is laid, it is the director's task to give the film its style. The many artistic details are born through his initiative. It ought to be his feelings and moods that color the film and that awaken corresponding feelings and moods in the spectator's mind. Through the style he infuses the work with a soul—and that is what makes it art. It is for him to give the film a face—namely his own.

Because it is like this, we directors have a very large responsibility. We have it in our hands to lift the film from industry to art, and, therefore, we must go to our work with seriousness, we must *want* something, we must *dare* something, and we must not jump over where the fence is lowest. If film as an art is not to come to a standstill, we must work to create a mark of style, a mark of personality in the film. Only from this can we expect renewal.

And I shall now give an account of some of the factors that have been decisive for the style in *Day of Wrath,* and I shall begin to talk about pictures and rhythm.

Sound films have an inclination to push pictures to the side and give the spoken words priority. In many of the sound films there is talk; no—*chatter*—all too much, while the eyes are seldom given permission to rest on a good picture effect. Meanwhile, film people have forgotten that the film first and foremost is a visual art, first and foremost directs itself to the eye, and that the picture far, *far* more easily than the spoken word penetrates deeply into the spectator's consciousness. I have in *Day of Wrath* tried to give the picture the place that it again should have, but yet not more. I don't bring a picture just for the sake of the picture, just because it's beautiful; if the picture effect does not promote the action it is injurious to the film.

The picture has a very great effect upon the spectator's state of mind. If it is kept in light tones, then it tunes the mind in a light way. If it is kept in dark, subdued tones, then it tunes the mind to seriousness. As was suitable to the time and the action in *Day of Wrath,* my photographer and I agreed to have the pictures veiled in soft grey and black tones.

The eye prefers order, and therefore it is of importance that the picture effects are harmonious and remain so even in movement. Ungraceful lines push the spectator's eye.

The eye absorbs horizontal lines rapidly and easily but repels vertical lines. The eye is involuntarily attracted by objects in motion but remains passive over stationary things. This is the explanation why the eye, with pleasure, follows gliding camera movements, preferably when they are soft and rhythmic. As a principle rule, one can say that one shall try to keep a continuous, flowing, horizontally gliding motion in the film. If one then suddenly introduces vertical lines, one can by this reach an instantly dramatic effect—as, for instance, in the pictures of the vertical ladder just before it is thrown into the fire in *Day of Wrath.*

Rhythm

Now we come to rhythm. The sound film in the last few years has conscientiously worked toward a new, specific sound-film rhythm. I think especially of a number of important foreign, style-marked films—the American, for one, and then also the good French psychological films. There is an aim in these films for a quietness in the rhythm that makes it possible for the spectator to rest on the pictures and listen to the words. But rightly so for these films, for it was also characteristic of them that their pictures were worth seeing and their words worth hearing.

I have tried to work further in the same line. In some action—for example, the scene in *Day of Wrath* between the two young people by Absalon's coffin—instead of using short, quick, shifting pictures, I introduced what I call long, gliding close-ups that follow the players in a rhythmic way, feeling their way from one to another just as the action is taking place with one and then the other. In spite of—or perhaps, more correctly, I should say because of—

HORIZONTAL/VERTICAL. *Day of Wrath*. Anna Svierkier as Herlof's Marthe being readied for burning as a witch.

HORIZONTAL/VERTICAL. *Day of Wrath.* "Backgrounds you feel more than see."

HORIZONTAL/VERTICAL. Frame blow-up from *Day of Wrath*.

this almost wave-formed rhythm, the scene with the two young people by Absalon's coffin is one of the parts that touches the public most strongly.

It has become a reproach to me that the rhythm in *Day of Wrath* is too heavy and too slow.

I have often seen a fast rhythm used with great effect in film—where such a rhythm was right for the situation. But I have also seen films where the pictures were whipped up by an artificial rhythm that was uncalled for by the action: it was a rhythm for the sake of the rhythm itself. But used this way, the rhythm is actually just an inheritance from the time of the silent films, an inheritance that the sound film still hasn't shaken off. It is a remnant from the time when film was fitted out with printed remarks. Between the remarks, it was empty, and the remarks were also empty, and in order to cover up all this emptiness the persons *flew* through the pictures and the pictures *flew* past on the screen—there was certainly "rhythm" enough! But *such* was the rhythm of the silent film.

When the Danish silent film was at its highest point—that was at least twenty-five years ago—some very remarkable films started to come from Sweden, the Selma Lagerlöf films. I remember clearly when Victor Sjöstrom's film, *The Sons of Ingermann,* was shown for the first time in Copenhagen. The film people here at home shook their heads because Sjöstrom had really a boldness to let his farmers walk heavily and soberly as farmers do. Yes, they used up an eternity to come from one end of the room to the other.

As I mentioned, the Danish film people shook their heads: it would never go over well; the audience would never accept it. But we all know how it went. It became the Swedish film with its natural, living rhythm that won not only in Sweden and Denmark but over all of Europe. All of Europe learned about the Swedish film—learned, among other things, that a film's rhythm was born from the action and the environment in the film. In this way, a very important interaction is created, because the drama creates a rhythm that in its turn supports the mood of the action at the same time that it influences the viewer's state of mind, so that he much more easily identifies with the drama itself.

It is the action and milieu in *Day of Wrath* that has decided its wide, quiet rhythm, but this also serves other aims: partly to underline the slow pulse of the ear, and, partly, to emphasize and support the monumentality the writer has aimed at in his play and that I have tried to carry over into the film.

The Drama

In all art, human beings are the decisive thing. In the artistic film, it is the people that we want to see and it is their adventures of the spirit that we want to experience. We want to enter upon and into the lives we see on the screen. We hope that the film will set ajar for us a door into these other worlds. We want to be placed in a suspense that originates less from outside action than from the unfolding of the inner conflicts. There is no lack of mental or spiritual conflict in *Day of Wrath*. On the other hand, one would search long for material more tempting for presentation as exterior drama. I—and, I dare to say, also my actors along with me—have chosen not to fall for the temptation. We have been just as eager in searching out the false exaggerations and the establishing cliches. We forced ourselves to search for truthfulness.

And isn't the truth that the great dramas are played quietly, that people try to cover their feelings and avoid showing on their faces the storms that are really raging within themselves? The tension lies beneath the surface and releases itself the day the catastrophe takes place. It is that latent tension, that smoldering discomfort behind the minister's family's everyday life that I have so urgently been trying to bring forward.

It is perhaps not enough for those who might have wished a more violent unfolding of the action. But let them look around their own circles and notice with how little of the dramatic the greatest tragedies take place. This is perhaps what is most tragic about these tragedies.

I am sure there are also some who would much rather have had the scenes more realistically elaborated. But realism in itself is not art; it is only psychological or spiritual realism that is so. What has value is the artistic truth, i.e., the truth distilled from actual life but released from all unnecessary details—the truth filtered through an artist's mind. What happens on the screen is not reality, and it cannot be so, because, if it was, it wouldn't be art.

With this point of view, I and my actors in good company have tried to *un-theatricalize* the film in itself from the very many tight and condensed scenes. Before I continue, I would like to define the difference between theatrical and filmic, and I would like to indicate that from my side I am not trying to put down in any way or sound derogative in using the word theatrical. I should like only to say that an actor can play differently on a theatre stage than in a film studio. On stage he must calculate that the words have to go completely over the orchestra seats and up into the galleries. This requires not only very good voice quality and diction but also that the facial expressions must be coarsened to go over this distance, whereas in a film studio all that is needed is the very ordinary daily language and the completely natural gesture. In the film *Day of Wrath,* we have not made any special effort to act more or less strong, more or less subdued. No, we have taken pains to play truthfully, to create live, believable persons. We have warned each other against falseness and pure exteriority.

Acting

A film actor's most important means of expression are gesture and speech.

When the sound film first came forward, gestural expression was set in the background. Now one had the spoken word. And the words gushed forth from the empty faces. In the French and American psychological films of recent years, facial expression is again brought to honor and given value, and it is all to the good. This kind of mime is an important element for the spoken film. Gesture endows the face with soul, and facial expression is an extra-important plus to the spoken word. We can often read a person's whole character in a single expression, a wrinkling of the forehead or a blink of the eye. Mime is the original means of expression of inner experience—older than the spoken word. Facial expression is not reserved for people only. If you have a dog, you will know that a dog can have a very expressive face.

While we are talking about facial expression, I should like to say a couple of words about makeup. To keep from losing the slightest little bit of a facial expression, I have also in the film *Day of Wrath* completely done away with made-up faces. When you look at what is usually done, the reality is this: the actor makes himself up for the photographer and the photographer therefore places the lights in a special way so that one doesn't see the makeup. People today, however, have learned to see beauty in the natural face with all of its furrows and wrinkles. If a face is covered with makeup, some of its character will be smoothened out. The wrinkles in a face, small as well as large, tell you endlessly much about the character. With a hearty, friendly, always-smiling man there will form over the years a number of fine wrinkles around his eyes and mouth. The wrinkles smile to us from a distance when we meet. If the man, on the other hand, is sour, evil, or cross, he gets wrinkles on his forehead and vertical furrows. In both cases the wrinkles tell us a little about the man inside the face. If one takes the makeup and tries to cover up the wrinkles, he is also hiding part of the characteristics of the man that the face would otherwise show us. I don't think I need to point out how important this is in close photography.

To produce a film in which the actors have absolutely no makeup —*Day of Wrath,* for instance—is only natural and obviously correct. And there lies in the whole spirit of film the truthful presentation that can only be reached with un-made-up actors who speak a very daily language.

Makeup and Diction

Makeup and diction both belong to the values of the theatre.

Carl Alstrup was once asked if he wouldn't like to go to the Royal Theatre in Copenhagen. He said that he didn't really want to, that for him, he also explained, "one cannot stand and scream and also be human." Alstrup gives just a glimpse of the problems theatre actors have to struggle with. At the same time, his observation quite strikingly tells us the deepest meaning of the word "filmic." This is the great advantage of the film over the theatre— that the actor can let his voice rest in natural position; yes, he can whisper if the role demands it. The microphone will certainly record it. Each word and each little pause can come into its own. But just because of this one shouldn't use unnecessary words. The spoken word should not play a self-standing role. It must be in accord with the nature of the drama, a constituent part of the picture, and this is how it should be. It must especially not be rambling. The dialogue must be condensed and concentrated as much as possible.

In choosing the actors, the spoken film's director must pay much attention to the voices. It is very important that they are tuned after each other and that they harmonize together. In this connection, I should like to say a little about something that the director must also think about. And it might be something new for you, namely, that there is a certain accordance between a human being's walk and speech. Just look at Lisbeth Movin: there is the finest coordination between the rhythm of her walk and the rhythm of her voice.

This has been a parenthetical comment, and I come now to the director's real and most decisive task, namely: the interaction with the players. If one wishes to find an image that portrays the director's action, one must compare him to a midwife. This is exactly the picture Stanislavski used in his book on actors and it absolutely couldn't be better. The actor is truly in labor and the director takes care of him, does everything he can to make the birth easier. The *child* is in the deepest sense the actor's own child, hatched from his own feelings and from his own inner life after his encounter with the writer's words. It is always his own emotion that the actor gives the role.

Therefore, the director is careful never to force his own interpretation on an actor, because an actor cannot create truth and pure emotions on command. One cannot push feelings out. They have to arise from themselves, and it is the director's and the actor's work in unison to bring them to that point. If this is successful the right expressions will come by themselves.

For the serious actor, it is a very great commandment that he must never start with the expression from the outside, but with the emotion from the inside. But just because emotion and expression are inseparably united, just because they make a unit, one can

BY DREYER POSSESSED. *Day of Wrath*. Lisbeth Movin as Anne. ". . . in each simple act there is only *one* expression which is the right one . . ."

BY DREYER POSSESSED. *Day of Wrath*. Thorkild Roose as Absalon.
". . . only *one single one*. To reach this—there is no more delightful
feeling for the director and actor . . ."

. . . AND DISPOSSESSED. Two regularly fine performers, Wanda Roth-
gart and Georg Rydeberg, miscast by the producers in the film Dreyer
"took back": *Two Lives* (1944).

sometimes with luck go the opposite way, i.e., start with the expression and thus call forth the feeling. I can better illustrate what I mean with an example. Imagine a little boy who is very angry with his mother. Then she kindly says to him, "Come on, smile a little." He smiles first an awkward, stiff smile, which, however, soon is followed by a big, open smile. A little bit later, he runs happily around. The anger is gone. One sees that the first smile has acted on the feeling which again has acted on the expression. It is this play of interaction one sometimes can build on. If it is easy for an actor to cry—there are those people for whom it is— it is justifiable to give the tears a free outburst without waiting for the *right* feeling; for the physical sensation that follows the cry will help the actor in the work of bringing forward the right feeling that in its turn then gives rise to the right expression—the *only* right expression, because in each simple act there is only *one* expression that is the right one, only *one single one.* To reach this— there is no more delightful feeling for the director and actor than when this works out.

Music

I cannot talk about film without saying a couple of words about music. It is Heinrich Heine who has said that where the words come out short there the music begins. This is just the task of the music. Correctly used, it is both capable of supporting the psychological development and of deepening a frame of mind that has been previously produced either through the pictures or through the dialogue. When the music really has meaning or an artistic intention, it will always be a plus for the film. But we must, nonetheless, hope for—and work to bring forth—more and more spoken films that have not the need of music, film in which the words do not come out short.

I have, as concretely as it has been possible for me to do, described the technical and spiritual processes that are decisive for the style of a film and have been so for *Day of Wrath.* I confess that I have talked much about technique but I'm not ashamed that I take the trouble to learn my job and know it from its foundations. Each artist knows that the first condition for him ever to become something as an artist is that he know his trade. But no one who has seen my film can doubt that technique for me is a means and not the goal and that the goal has been to give the spectator a *richer* experience.

My Only Great Passion (1950)

In these excerpts from a radio interview for the program "New Perspectives on the Arts and Science," broadcast October 23, 1950, Dreyer begins by commenting on the irony of having been accused of committing certain anachronisms in *Joan of Arc.* It was not the only time that Dreyer's authenticity would make him prey to carpers more concerned with upstaging the artist than verifying sources. Extraneities and inaccuracies—*invariably in the name of the essential and true*—were directed at Dreyer throughout his career, reaching a crescendo with the appearance of *Gertrud* and its reception by the daily reviewers.

Getting underway in the interview, Dreyer again puts forth one of the cornerstones of his aesthetic position: ". . . realism, in itself, is not art . . ." But then he qualifies this with one of the most succinct delineations of the *Lumière-Méliès ratio* on record: ". . . there must be a harmony between the genuineness of *feelings* and the genuineness of *things* . . ." Here is an expansion of (the late) Marianne Moore's "imaginary gardens with real toads" to include its converse as well. In the interview Dreyer calls this *"psychological realism"* and mentions how he strives for it through a kind of simplification and abbreviation that, in later years, became his principle of "abstraction." But this earlier comment on "psychological realism" and the relationship between *feelings* and *things* within such a context sheds morning light on the evolution of his theory and practice of cinematic consciousness. It bears closely upon the developing and deepening style of his films: Through simplification Dreyer eliminated the less essential materials of his scenes and arrived at a heightened presence of those elements belonging to, and in turn generating, a state of selective awareness. And he managed to do this within a narrative framework—*Day of Wrath, Ordet, Gertrud*—which in the hands of

143

lesser artists tends to swallow images whole and serve them back to the viewer as *concepts* rather than *percepts*. Only Robert Bresson—different from Dreyer in so many ways—seems to have resolved this have-your-cake-and-eat-it paradox of cinema—story momentum versus graphic presence—to the same degree.

Organic to Dreyer's general filmic sense of "psychological realism" is his presentation of character. Here, too, there is "simplification" but not into the polarities of black and white. Rather, it is a simplification that ranges the entire gray scale of human personality from black to white, distilling to essentials along the way so that the character has uniquely real facets that resonate through interaction with other equally "whole" characters and the total *mise-en-scène* as well. This is particularly true about the scenario for the unmade Jesus film, which Dreyer had recently returned from writing in the United States. His preoccupation with a balanced view of even the most mythically villainous characters will be treated in a section on the Jesus film, a bit later in this book.

About Joan of Arc *Dreyer said:*

I had given the English soldiers who attended the trial against Joan of Arc steel helmets to wear, and several critics resented that. But the truth is that the fifteenth century's soldiers actually wore steel helmets that were exactly like the ones English soldiers wore during the First World War. The same critics also made a fuss because one of the monks in the film wore horn-rimmed glasses, which, in 1927 [when the film was made], were very much in fashion. But I could produce miniatures that prove that people in the fifteenth century wore horn-rimmed glasses just like the ones that were used when the film was made. In the miniatures we also found a scenery style that was content to *suggest* the era without imposing itself. I have followed the same principle in *Day of Wrath,* and I am also going to follow it in my film on Christ. For since realism, in itself, is not art, and since, on the other hand, there must be harmony between the genuineness of *feelings* and the genuineness of *things,* I try to force the realities into a form of simplification and abbreviation in order to reach what I will call *psychological realism.*

The interviewer asked if Dreyer, despite the "timelessness" in his films, was not strongly tied to the time in which we live, and Dreyer answered:

Concerning *Joan of Arc* and *Day of Wrath,* I will reply that one never knows, of course, what goes on in one's subconsciousness, but as for the film on Christ, there is probably something to what you say. The first time I thought of the Gospels as material for a film was some time after I had finished *Joan of Arc* and I was looking for a long time for a point from which I could see the Gospels at an angle different from the traditional one. A couple of days after the 9th of April 1940, it suddenly struck me that the Jews in Palestine must have had it like we now had it ourselves—only that it was Romans instead of Germans and a Pilate instead of a Renthe-Fink. A closer study showed several parallels. Among other things, the Jews also had their underground movement: young patriotic Jews—called "Zealots"—who attacked outlying Roman garrisons and set fire to Jewish collaborationists' houses and fields.

About "impartiality" in the films:

. . . In both *Joan of Arc* and *Day of Wrath* I have consciously tried to remain impartial. The clergy in the two films did indeed condemn Joan and the harmless old witch to the stake, but it was not because they were evil and cruel. They were only caught up in the religious conceptions of that time. When they tortured their victims in order to force a confession from them, it was because the confession insured the accused eternal life.

About the public:

Apart from the fact that I naturally take the trouble to organize my material so that the audience can easily grasp it, I must be honest and say that beyond that I don't have the public in my thoughts for one moment. Consciously, I don't do anything to "please" the public. I only think of working my way to a solution that satisfies my own artistic conscience. And I believe, you know, that this is the right way to work. At least I have had the experience in a couple of cases where, forced or voluntarily, I did compromise and it was only detrimental to me.

Why does Dreyer feel drawn to tragedy?

Because I find it easier in tragedy to work in my own personality and my own outlook [on life]—to introduce this "something" that makes people listen, this "something" that points beyond the film itself, this "something" that, to use a worn-out phrase, people "go home with."

Is there an inclination in the film about Jesus?

Yes, there is insofar as I think it will help to straighten out the antagonisms between Christians and Jews. For this reason, among others, I want to let Jesus be represented as a Jew. The masses have a deeply rooted conception that Jesus was blond and Aryan. It is a good turn, I think, to see to it that this prejudice is stamped out.

Should the film director himself write the script?

The ideal is, of course, that the director writes his own manuscript. He first becomes a *creating* artist (as opposed to a *reproducing* artist) in the deeper sense (only) when he has written his manuscript himself. Then he is not only an attendant in the service of another vision. The manuscript has come into existence under the pressure of an inner drive to write *just this* film. And since he himself gives the film both content and form, he thereby insures its intimate dramatic and psychological coherence.

At last, the interviewer asked: "What is film to you?", and Dreyer replied:

My only great passion.

Who Crucified Jesus? (1951)

Dreyer's dislike of propaganda—made clear in the earlier essay on the Soviet Gulliver film—tended to take the edge off any *message*-thrust his films might have had. He was much more concerned with the distilled objectification of his vision of the human condition than with championing a particular cause. He called this "art," as opposed to "propaganda," and although he had a stylistic inclination toward *simplifying,* he never oversimplified the complex circumstances out of which even the most potentially *villainous* of his characters was forced to operate. At the same time, many of his most sympathetic characters—heroes and heroines, if you will—were shown to have flaws or weaknesses that brought them within human reach of their less sympathetic adversaries. Dreyer generated intense fields of dramatic energy in these narrowed gaps between his characters, especially in the later films—between Martin and Absalon, and even Anne and Merete in *Day of Wrath;* between Borgen, the patriarch, and each of his troubled children—and Peter the tailor, in *Ordet.* And the effect becomes most quicksilver in *Gertrud* through the interaction of wife, lover, old friend, and old flame. One has the choice of keeping up with Dreyer's nimbleness or pigeonholing things more conveniently (and conventionally) into stock roles and situations.

Because of this, too, the question of "realized mysticism" is the least resolved and most confusing in the mind of that part of his audience that *almost* accepts Dreyer and *almost* responds to the majority of his films. Dreyer's writings on his unmade Jesus film provide clarification of the backgrounds and motives out of which his filmmaking tended to grow.

In this essay, which appeared in *Politiken* October 28, 1951, the crux of "realized mysticism" emerges more clearly than ever before. Dreyer is excited by Dr. Zeitlin's book on the Crucifixion because it seems to penetrate through to very earthly realities concerning the events that led up to Christ's death. Fact and spirit enhance each other for Dreyer, and by guiding himself with details that have the ring of truth to them, he avoids the confusion and vagueness that much *un*realized mysticism conveys. In the scenario itself, notice how he resolves the question of Jesus' nature and sense of mission:

Jesus never publicly proclaimed himself the Messiah but undoubtedly he had slowly reached the conclusion that he was the expected Messiah, called by God to establish his Kingdom on Earth. But Jesus felt that his mission in the world was an infinitely higher one than just to fulfill the traditionally national and political hopes that were tied to the Messianic dream of the people. Jesus wanted a revolution, but one of a spiritual nature. And he gave the Messiahship a new significance by identifying it with "the righteous servant" of whom Isaiah had spoken and who through his sufferings would redeem Israel.

When, therefore, he decided the next day to enter the Holy City, he wished by a symbolic act to emphasize that he came as a Messiah in a spiritual sense, but the multitude thought of the Messiah only in political and military terms.

The "otherworldliness" that some viewers associate with Dreyer's films is, for the most part, a fusion of his deeply accurate observations of human action and interaction presented through authentically cinematic techniques, refined by the director over many years, which heighten the sense of presence of whatever state of being Dreyer attempts to communicate and evoke. It is by *discarding* "otherworldly" pretensions that Dreyer arrives at this and that his characters achieve their "grace"—a process made explicit in *Ordet,* which is Dreyer's fable on this very point. And the character of Judas, as Dreyer drew it for the Jesus film, becomes archetypal of the individual incapable of resolving, of fusing the earthly and the spiritual into one, as Dreyer's own description shows:

In the beginning [Judas] had for Jesus sincere devotion and faith. But he was by nature a skeptic and after a while he began looking at Jesus with critical eyes. Not of a spiritual bent of mind, he interpreted the words of Jesus literally and he noticed with disapproval how often Jesus appeared to contradict himself. In the discussions between Jesus and the Pharisees, he often was inclined to agree with them rather than with Jesus, whose thought was beyond his comprehension.

After an invitation by the American theatre man, Blevins Davis, I came to the U.S.A. to work out a manuscript for a film on Jesus. I had naturally already formed my own theory regarding the events that must have preceded the arrest of Jesus. A couple of days after the Germans occupied Denmark, it struck me that such a situation as we were now in was the same situation that the Jews must have been in. The hatred we felt toward the Nazis the Jews must also have felt toward the Romans. Out of that recognition my theory had grown. I suspected that the capture, the conviction, and the death of Jesus in reality was the result of a conflict between Jesus and the Roman occupying power.

I was fortunate enough, right after my arrival in the U.S.A. to come across a book that had recently been published and which would agree with me. Its title was *Who Crucified Jesus?* The author was Dr. Solomon Zeitlin, professor in the Rabbinical Department at Dropsie College in Philadelphia—a Jewish scholar of international reputation. But before I can go into the new viewpoints that Dr. Zeitlin puts forward in his book, I have got to mention the Jewish people's attitude toward the occupying power.

The Roman governor Pilate was the real master in the country. Opposite him but appointed by him, the high priest Caiaphas stood as the responsible leader of the Jewish population. Besides holding the high-priestly office, Caiaphas was also the Jewish state's secular chief. He and the upper class established a "wait-and-see" policy toward the Romans, a policy aimed at procuring for the population of the country as tolerable conditions as possible by negotiating to get along with the Roman masters. The Romans (like the Germans in this country), in order to obligate the Jews, granted them certain privileges such as religious freedom, municipal self-government, their own police and their own courts—except in cases that concerned the safety of the state, i.e., the Romans, in which cases they reserved the right to pass sentence and execute punishment.

In the middle of the desperation over living as a suppressed people, the Jews never gave up the hope that a Jewish kingdom would rise again when the Messiah, predicted by the prophets, some day would be born. They imagined this Messiah as a great warrior and general who would revenge Israel and chase the Romans into the sea. Hoping this, the common man picked up strength and courage to bear the Roman yoke.

However, there were some people who did not bear their sufferings with the same patience and preferred to meet terror with terror. They united in a sect, the Sicarii, and initiated guerrilla war against the Romans. Time and again their attempts at rebellion were crushed but they did not give up. They also pursued those of their countrymen who fraternized with the Romans, among them some of the great landowners who let the Romans have their grain. The Sicarii maintained that such Jews—corresponding to our own "collaborationists"—were to be regarded as traitors, and they burned their crops or "liquidated" them without pity. The Sicarii, without further ado, can be compared to our own Resistance people.

Dr. Zeitlin mentions still another sect, called the Apocalyptic Pharisees. They, too, were hoping for a revolutionary change of society but thought that the people would be liberated by God's direct intervention. They probably imagined the coming Messiah as descending from David's family but gifted with supernatural abilities.

Knowledge of the beliefs and activities of these two sects is a prerequisite for understanding the attitude that the Romans must have had to take toward Jesus. A few days before his entry into Jerusalem, Jesus had, in Bethany right outside Jerusalem, awakened Lazarus from the dead. And in Jerusalem itself, Jesus cured a man who had been lame for thirty-eight years and a young man who had been born blind. The lame could walk and the blind could see: Was Jesus perhaps the Messiah with the supernatural powers that the Apocalyptic Pharisees were raving about? One thing is certain: the Romans kept a watchful eye both on the Sicarians and on the Apocalyptic Pharisees and did not distinguish between them but regarded them as dangerous rebels to an equally high degree and crucified them in great number.

Let us now consider for a moment what Dr. Zeitlin has to tell us about the Jewish Council that Jesus was brought before after his arrest in the Gethsemane Garden. One will remember that Mark, Luke, and John each mention that Jesus was taken to the high priest's house and there put before "a council of elders and scribes." What kind of council was this?

From old times, there existed a council that was called the great Sanhedrin. It consisted of seventy-one members, was a legislative council whose exclusive task was to interpret the Biblical law, establish the calendar year, and the like.

Apart from this "great council," there was another "smaller council"—the little Sanhedrin. It was composed of twenty-three members who had authority to judge in cases of crimes against religious laws and also in crimes that implied capital punishment, like murder, incest, public profanation of the Sabbath, and blasphemy. The little Sanhedrin had meetings every day of the week except Saturday and holidays—*and days that preceded such days.* This had its special reason. Although the Romans without scruple passed death sentences in assembly-line fashion, the Jews were very humane in their court practice. They avoided a sentence to death for as long as possible. A man could be acquitted the same day he was brought before the council as accused. But he could not be *sentenced to death* before the next day. A death sentence was not to be pronounced inconsiderately. And even after the death sentence was pronounced, the case could be taken up to new trial if new information, regardless of where it came from, was presented in favor of the condemned man. Yes, so far went the Jewish judges' dread of executing an innocent human being that when the person several times sentenced to death was at last taken to the place of execution, a court officer headed the procession carrying a tablet on a long stick. The tablet had an inscription that urged everyone who possessed information that might be favorable to the condemned man to appear immediately at the council. If anybody reported, the execution was postponed and the case taken up again. Since Jesus was crucified the day before Passover, it cannot have been the little Sanhedrin to which Jesus was taken after his arrest in Gethsemane Garden, since the little Sanhedrin, as mentioned, did not meet on days before a holiday. They never held meetings at night either.

What sort of council was it, then, that Jesus stood face-to-face with in the high priest's house?

Dr. Zeitlin solves this riddle by explaining that as long as Judea had been independent, a third, a "political" Sanhedrin existed besides the two "religious" Sanhedrins, which took care of those who offended the state or its chief. The members of this political Sanhedrin were appointed by the chief of state, who, of course, chose only those persons as members whom he knew would dance to his tune. When Judea became a Roman province, the Romans took over the administration of justice when political crimes were concerned. Now, as mentioned earlier, the high priest was responsible for social and political order in Judea and it was his duty to arrest every one of his countrymen who could be suspected of rebellious intentions. When this happened, the person involved was brought before the high priest and a council consisting of his closest confidants and advisors. This council was an imitation of the political Sanhedrins of earlier times.

It had no right to sentence the accused, only to hear him and examine prospective witnesses' statements, after which his case was submitted to the Roman governor, who passed sentence and let the punishment be carried out.

Dr. Zeitlin draws attention to the fact that, in all the cases which are known, the practice was that first the accused was arrested and then the political council was summoned. And this was precisely how it happened in the case of Jesus. Dr. Zeitlin further states that this political council held their meetings at any time of the day and, if circumstances demanded it, even at night, and it had not any definite meeting place, as opposed to the two religious

Sanhedrins. From this, Dr. Zeitlin asserts, it can be concluded that it was to this political council that Jesus had been taken at night after having been arrested.

If this theory is true, then Jesus was treated as a political criminal; but was there really reason to consider Jesus a rebel and a person dangerous to the state?

In order to answer this question, Dr. Zeitlin reminds us that when Jesus made his entry into Jerusalem he was cheered as "David's Son" and greeted with the cry: "Blessed be our father David's kingdom that comes."

What was behind these cheers?

The old prophets who spoke in God's name and whose words were preserved by oral tradition had predicted that a man of David's line would some day come as a Messiah, sent by God and, as chosen by God, make himself king of the Jews.

So Jesus, at his entry into Jerusalem, was not only cheered as David's son, he was also greeted with shouts like "Blessed be *the king* who comes in the name of the Lord" (Mark), and "Hosanna, blessed be the one who comes in the name of the Lord, the king of Israel" (John).

By letting himself be cheered as Messiah, David's son and king of Israel, Jesus not only incurred the Romans' suspicion of being an accomplice of revolutionary groups within the Jewish population but his entry was in itself a direct challenge to the Romans and to be regarded as a rebellious action that entitled them to demand that Jesus be handed over. Further, after his entry, Jesus immediately began to chase from the courtyard of the temple the stockbrokers and those who traded in sacrificial animals; this was such a breach of social order that both the Romans and the responsible Jewish authorities, in keeping with their whole attitude, were necessarily filled with resentment. Seen with the eyes of those last-mentioned, it was simply the welfare of the Jewish people that Jesus risked by his conduct.

According to Dr. Zeitlin, the high priest could not, therefore, do anything else but have Jesus arrested, interrogated in the presence of the political council, and then—when Jesus confessed that he regarded himself as Messiah—hand him over to Pilate.

As my own personal opinion, I consider it just as possible that it was the Romans who demanded Jesus arrested and handed over; for the Romans, who commanded a well-organized "Gestapo," were of course carefully informed of all that went on in Judea, especially in Jerusalem during the Passover. We had in this country [Denmark]—*sans comparaison*—an almost analogous case from the time of the Occupation when the Germans, on February 24, 1942, requested and got Wilh. la Cour handed over. I think it follows from Caiaphas' remarks, cited in John, that matters could have been as suggested: "Ye know nothing at all, nor consider that it is expedient for us, that one man should die for the people and that the whole nation perish not." The fretful, snappish tone seems to indicate that Caiaphas, even within the narrow political council, had met resistance against the handing over of Jesus from the advisors, who otherwise were probably puppets in his hand. This is, however, a purely personal opinion.

When Jesus was brought before Pilate the next morning, the first question the Roman governor put to him was this: "Are you 'King of the Jews,' " to which Jesus gave the evasive answer: "You say so [Thou sayest]." From this, too, Dr. Zeitlin draws the conclusion that Jesus was really handed over to the Romans as a political criminal who had committed an offense against the Roman state. The point in the accusation that interested Pilate probably was this: that Jesus aspired to become king of the Jews.

When I had finished my manuscript and had drawn knowledge from Dr. Zeitlin's inspiring book, I had the pleasure of getting to know the writer personally. Blevins Davis managed to lure the learned man out of his study and persuaded him to read my manuscript and go through it critically with me. The collaboration was a great experience and, for my part, very fruitful. It was he, of course, who talked and I who listened. We ended up agreeing on all points except one. Dr. Zeitlin, in his book, is very harsh on Caiaphas, whom he repeatedly describes as a "quisling." I don't think he was that. One may call him a "collaborating politician" but definitely not a "quisling." There is, in my humble opinion, nothing that indicates that Caiaphas was not a well-meaning man who had the people's well-being in his thoughts. He was a realistic politician, and as such he considered it wisest for the Jewish people to go easy in order not to lose the little freedom that was left them. So the designation "quisling" is not only unjust but also incorrect— if only because of the deep gulf between Jewish and Roman "ideology." For the Romans, religion was subordinated to the state; for the Jews, religion stood above the state—religion was everything. And so I have gone my own way regarding the Caiaphas character in my manuscript—but otherwise I am deeply grateful to Dr. Zeitlin, who, I think, has reached the goal he set himself: to refute the accusation against the Jews for having murdered Jesus. This infamous charge was stated for the first time during the first century after Jesus' death. It is that long ago. Anti-Semitism is that old. We all know what this infamy has brought the Jews in sorrow and tears, suffering and death.

The Cinematization of *Ordet* (*The Word*) (1954)

Dreyer became more boldly experimental with each film he made. To make things even more difficult—in terms of reaching a general audience—his experiments were not *overtly* adventurous or signaled by technical flamboyance. Rather, Dreyer undertook projects that delineated more and more subtle states of being and human interaction. From *The Passion of Joan of Arc* (1928) through *Gertrud* (1964), each Dreyer film becomes, increasingly, an exercise in the refinement of sensibility and consciousness. Only *Gertrud* can be considered a more difficult film than *Ordet* (1955) and in certain respects *Ordet* presents greater problems. Certainly *Ordet* is the culminating film dealing directly with the questions of personal and organized religion so closely identified with Dreyer from *Joan of Arc* on. And it is in *Ordet* that Dreyer presents his most striking instance of "realized mysticism," a moment of resurrection that seems to have left even previously sympathetic viewers far behind.

The interview that follows—the transcript of a radio broadcast —has a revealing subtext. Dreyer talks about his attempts at resolving a connection between "exact science and intuitive religion" and he also refers to the ambiguity of one of the characters in *Ordet,* Johannes. Neither of these issues is presented as a dualism in the film, but rather as a uniquely unified entity. The unification cannot be presented through literary modes with the same directness and immediacy—even simultaneity—that cinema allows. It is this specifically cinematic capacity that Dreyer works to refine and strengthen: there are organic ambiguities, simultaneities of even opposing meanings that can occur on screen in a way not possible on page, or stage for that matter. This is at the heart of the overriding paradox embodied in Dreyer's movies: that some of the most intrinsically cinematic films ever made were based upon material originated for other media. Dreyer sheds light on this in the interview, too. He speaks of his efforts at *simplification,* particularly of elements not essentially filmic. Systematically reducing extraneities throughout the entire creative process leading to the completion of his film, Dreyer moves the essentials, the primary elements of the *work-as-cinema* into the foreground of the field of consciousness it objectifies. The end result of this process can seem blandly simple, even devitalized, to the viewer seeking literary or theatrical inroads to the action— *handles* that Dreyer has made an effort to remove. This approach, as it occurs in *Ordet,* is still best referred to as *simplification;* in *Gertrud* it is, more accurately, the *abstraction* that Dreyer uses as an alternate term when describing this technique. But simplification permeates *Ordet* at all levels of its realization. It is in the settings and decor, in the acting (in varying degrees among the performances), and in the camerawork and editing, too, as Dreyer's replies to the interviewer reflect rather incisively.

A function of this simplification is Dreyer's method with actors. Surface nuance is extraneity to Dreyer, as the earlier essay on Jannings showed. The mannered performance is a *conceptual* event rather than a perceptual one, and the concept is usually drawn from literary or theatrical modes and necessities. It is Dreyer's awareness of film's capacity to absorb and reflect manifestations of inner life that led him to choose the actors who populate his movies. The performance of Emil Hass Christensen as Mikkel in *Ordet* is an exemplary instance of this. Apparently, it takes many viewings to appreciate fully the total *congruence* of actor and character, so organic and unmannered is his life on screen. But none of Christensens' past performances suggested the potentiality realized in *Ordet*—except, it would seem, to Dreyer.

I think that it is also worth noting Dreyer's own awareness of a certain simplification occurring in his montage technique. *The Passion of Joan of Arc* and *Vampyr* show a strong Eisensteinian influence; at least they are movies built film-piece by film-piece in accordance with the dynamic of juxtapositioning that was a hallmark of the Russian masterworks of the twenties. But, in *Day*

OUTSIDE THE FENCE OF NATURALISM. The resurrection scene in *Ordet*
(1955). "The primary elements of the *work as cinema*."

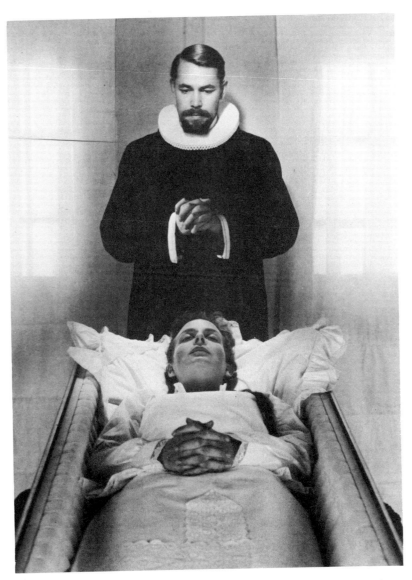

OUTSIDE THE FENCE OF NATURALISM. Birgitte Federspiel and Ove Rud in *Ordet*. "Transforming the work into a wholly cinematic entity."

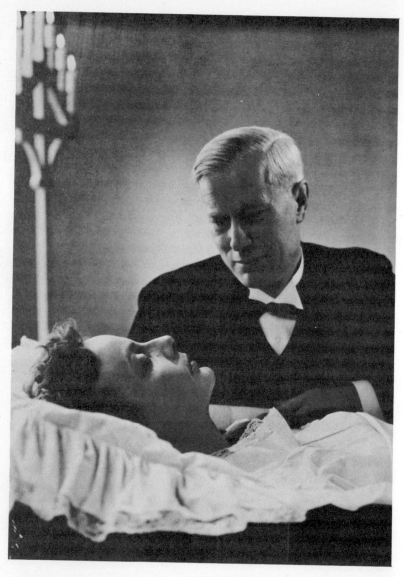

OUTSIDE THE FENCE OF NATURALISM. *Ordet*. Birgitte Federspiel and Emil Mass Christensen. ". . . accumulation of consciousness."

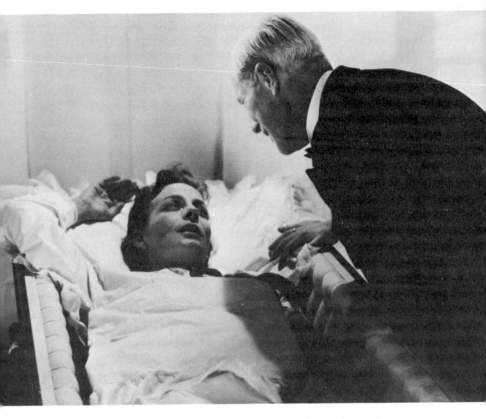

OUTSIDE THE FENCE OF NATURALISM. *Ordet*. The *right* performers *interacting*.

OUTSIDE THE FENCE OF NATURALISM. *Ordet*. Realized mysticism: the round trip from body to soul.

of Wrath, after nearly a decade without having made a feature film and—not insignificantly, I think—in the midst of the German Occupation of Denmark, 1943, Dreyer seemed to relax this highly manipulatory montage technique in favor of longer takes.

This tendency grew with each film that followed. _Ordet_ is built on long, flowing takes (as Dreyer, himself, called them). In a sense, Dreyer forfeited that edge of kineticism to be gained through the changes occurring from splice to splice, and at a superficial level, this undoubtedly contributes to the growing sense of stasis that some viewers point out as a deterrent to full involvement in his later works. But it is clear that Dreyer grew to prefer the _accumulation_ of consciousness within the unjostled sensibility of the viewer rather than the manipulation of that sensibility through bombardment from the screen. It is as if, in his last works, Dreyer had begun to work toward the generation of a new dimension of cinematic consciousness, a dimension dependent upon a depth-of-field of consciousness, achieved through an accumulation and deepening of charge, rather than the continual discharge of the viewer's attentive energies in accordance with a superficially gratifying pattern of rhythmic release.

Q. When did you first come to think of filming _Ordet?_
A. It happened one evening twenty-two years ago when I attended its first performance at the Betty Nansen Theatre. I was moved by the play and taken by surprise at the audacity with which Kaj Munk set the problems up against one another. I could not avoid being overcome with admiration for the apparent ease with which the writer presented his paradoxical assertions. As I left the theatre, I felt convinced that there was fine material for a film in that play.
Q. And, then, when was the film manuscript worked out?
A. Some twenty years went by before it happened. And at that point I saw Kaj Munk's ideas in a different light. For, in the inter-

val, so many things happened, you know. The new science that followed Einstein's theory of relativity had presented evidence that, outside the three-dimensional world that we can sense with our senses, there is both a fourth dimension—the dimension of time—and a fifth dimension—the dimension of the psychical. It was demonstrated as possible to experience occurrences that have not yet taken place. New perspectives were opened that make us realize a deep connection between exact science and intuitive religion. The new science brings us closer to a deeper understanding of the divine and is well on its way to giving a natural explanation for supernatural things. Kaj Munk's John [Johannes]-figure is now seen from a new angle. Kaj Munk already suspected this in 1925 when he wrote and suggested that the insane John is perhaps closer to God than are the Christians who surround him.

Q. Has it been difficult to adapt Kaj Munk for film?

A. It turned out to be not at all easy. One has to preserve Kaj Munk and at the same time free oneself from him. One must continually keep in mind what Kaj Munk wanted with his play and try to bring this out in the film. But also at the same time remember that Kaj Munk wrote for the theatre and that theatre has rules different from film. Situations and remarks that are effective from the stage often turn out to be deadly dangerous on film. A revaluation and simplification must take place. Actually, in the filming of a play, one could, I think, talk about a purification taking place, insofar as everything that doesn't promote the central idea must be removed. A condensation and a compression take place. The dialogue included in the film hardly amounts to more than a third of the play's original dialogue. This gives an impression of how thorough the simplification process must be. For film it holds true that a remark that is not understood immediately, in the same fraction of a second that it sounds forth from the screen, is a bad thing, because it stops the action. The audience must stop in order to make sense of what has been said. Therefore, even words that tend to be difficult to understand must be avoided. I can mention as an example Kaj Munk's use of the phrase "in Christ-the-grave-burster's name." It would be completely wrong to include a word like "grave-burster" in a film. In theatre there is always time to reflect, but not so on film. Before the spectator in the movie house gets around to figuring out what Kaj Munk meant by the word "grave-burster," the film will have come to the next scene without the spectator being able to follow.

Q. Do you follow your own manuscript slavishly during the shooting of a film?

A. The manuscript for a film should be regarded only as a rough draft that actors and director can work with further in the studio, where the purification and simplification are continued. One keeps on finding sentences again and again that are repetitions of things already said before—which is perfectly all right when it happens on stage but not when [the medium] is film. And if a Kaj Munk work is to be converted into film, then the goal must be to transform the work into a wholly cinematic entity. And my approach to working with Kaj Munk's *The Word* has, therefore, always been and still is this: first, to possess oneself of Kaj Munk and then forget him. At the same time, preserve him and free oneself from him. I have had the good fortune during the work that is involved in simplifying the manuscript, to find the greatest understanding with Mrs. Lise Munk. We have agreed that Kaj Munk himself very likely would have preferred a full-fledged Kaj Munk film rather than a screen version of a theatre piece. But whether I have reached this goal, time will show when the film is finished.

Q. And now the casting of roles?

A. It is really very important. With the right cast a film is already piloted halfway to shore. It is not only important that each actor be right for his role, he must also be right in relation to his fellow actors. One must believe that father and son and man and wife belong together. Therefore, one shall, I mean, not attach too much importance to the external similarity between role and actor. The *inner* similarity is the decisive issue—namely, similarity in regard to mentality, character, and temperament. I feel, for my part, that I have been lucky enough to find the right actors for all the roles, and there is not a single one of the roles that I should today wish to be differently cast.

Q. And the settings?

A. During my stay over by the North Sea, I found all around on the farms in the dune districts a rather overwhelming interest in the film and a quite unique generosity that found expression in the way that we were permitted to borrow furniture that had been standing in these farmhouses for several generations and paintings which are so typical of the homes in this part of the country. The rooms at the studio were furnished with all these things. Later on we took some of it away again in order to carry out a simplification, the purpose of which was to leave only the things that could contribute to characterizing the people the film dealt with.

Q. Your photography is world-famous.

A. I have always been lucky enough to find very capable photographers who understood my intentions, made them their own, and brought them to life. I myself do not understand photography in the least. I don't know anything about the relation between light and diaphragm, or about the relation between negative and positive. But I take a great deal of interest in film editing and picture composition, and I believe that the condition for good photography in general is a good collaboration between photographer and director. On this film, I am working together with a young, very gifted and talented photographer, Henning Bendtsen. We agreed that we wouldn't be satisfied with just good photography; what we would strive for was coming up with the right mood. In the old days, film photographers spoke about "laying light on." Today, one speaks about both "laying light on" and "laying darkness on." "Laying darkness on" is actually just as important as being able to "lay light on." A face that lies in darkness can, under certain circumstances, be more effective and express more than if it is in full light.

Q. In film, is photographic style tantamount to the style of a film?

A. Style is not only photography There are many concurrent factors that, combined, form the style, among other things the tempo and rhythm of the action. And the total rhythm of the film is again an amalgamation of many different rhythms, from the gliding camera right to the way the lines are read.

Q. Concerning the action, do you work much with your actors?

A. By and large, no. In *The Word* I am fortunate enough to work with actors who manage on their own to come up with the tone and mood that in my opinion are correct, and this is naturally the right thing. The actor's particular creative act must take place in the actor's own mind. Therefore, in my opinion, a film director's task is mainly to unite the single actor's achievements into a compositional whole.

Q. Have you changed your view of film rhythm since _Day of Wrath?_

A. Not really, although I have continued along the paths I turned to in _Day of Wrath._ Namely, with long scenes that are played through as opposed to scenes that are built up from many short, close-up pictures. In _Day of Wrath_ I called these gliding takes "flowing close-ups," and my view of their value hasn't changed. But I think it is dangerous, by the way, to maintain that one rhythmical form is better than another. All forms are useful when they are adapted to the character of the scenes they are to be used in, according to the rhythm of the action, the environment, and the intensity of the dramatic tension itself. As a matter of fact, one has to be cautious in talking about old-fashioned and modern rhythm, for the old-fashioned one can under certain circumstances be the most modern.

Color Film and Colored Film (1955)

Of all the films that he actually was given the chance to make, *Gertrud* is the only one that Dreyer envisaged in color (although, of course, he was eventually forced to make it in black-and-white). Interviewed in *Cahiers du Cinéma* in 1965, Dreyer commented that he had not thought about color for any of his films up to and including *Ordet.* But although it would be a full decade between *Ordet* and *Gertrud,* the article below, appearing originally in *Politiken,* February 27, 1955 (just a year after completion of *Ordet*), shows how involved with the problem of color film Dreyer actually was long before contemplating it as a possibility for *Gertrud.* It is likely that it entered his thoughts in connection with some of his long-standing and never-realized film projects—the Jesus film, for instance, for which he had completed a scenario as early as 1950.

The basic contention of the article is that although cinema had brought forth many "colored movies," *color film,* an art in itself as Dreyer saw it, had not yet been really achieved in other than a handful of instances. Dreyer sensed a dimension beyond the ordinary uses of color that had prevailed since its advent twenty years earlier. What he had in mind he himself makes amply clear. But his philosophy here seems to reflect his philosophy of black-and-white filmmaking as well: finding the deeper secrets and dynamics of the process in order to arrive at extraordinary effects. A careful reading of the paragraph that begins with "For the director, the colors are a valuable aid" reveals the incisive and comprehensive mind of this filmmaker and suggests the depth and diversity of energies at work below the seemingly simple surfaces of many of his greatest films and film moments.

Two other Dreyer convictions reappear in the course of his discussion of color: the paradox of cinema as both a deeply individualistic and at the same time highly collective art, and the question of naturalism versus artistic effect.

As personally stamped as all of Dreyer's films are, he nonetheless acknowledges his great dependence upon other craftsmen. In the case of color, he goes even further by calling for collaboration with craftsmen, technicians, *and* color *artists*. And he goes beyond the conventional role of the production designer by naming the painters he has in mind and the depth of responsibility he would assign to them. At the same time, he redefines the role of the director within such a framework in a way that increases rather than decreases his personal responsibility for arriving at a unified whole.

His renunciation of naturalism reaches a peak when Dreyer calls for green skies and blue grass, "just once." But here, too, is a reflection of his work in black-and-white. The apparent simplicity of his film style should not be confused with realism, in itself. Always at work is a subtle blending of realistic and formal tendencies—of Lumière and Méliès, as it were—leading to delicate but decisive abstractions. This is worth noting again and again, if for nothing else than as preparation for full receptivity to *Gertrud,* in which the daring balances of opposing elements— real/formal, tragic/comic—are seamlessly integral to the general weave of the piece.

This year it is twenty years since the first feature film in color came out. Hundreds of color films followed, but when we look back, how many of them do we remember for the aesthetic pleasure they gave us? Two—three—four—five? Maybe five, but probably not more. *Romeo and Juliet* just manages to be included in those five—after Olivier's *Henry V* and the Japanese Kinugasa's *Gate of Hell*. Olivier picked up the ideas for his choice of colors from miniatures of medieval manuscripts, while the Japanese director went back to his people's classical woodcut art. And beyond those, only "attempts at something"—best in *Moulin Rouge,* where the smoke-filled dance halls at the beginning compelled admiration, while all the rest was more on the level of the ordinary as far as color goes. And why? Because the director here did not have Toulouse-Lautrec to lean on. For, to be sure, the director who directed the film was great, but, as a painter, Toulouse-Lautrec was greater. But, really, four or five artistic feature films in color during the course of twenty years—a very modest result.

Apart from enjoyable and surprising color effects in musicals, rather cheap taste still prevails in the majority of feature films, which very likely is due to the fear of getting off the safe but boring ground of naturalism. Of course, one can find poetry in a slice of everyday life but a film in color doesn't become art by meticulously and precisely copying the colors of nature. For the feature film in color, the naturalistic attitude has, in any case, been a serious drawback. One sat watching the colors to see if they were really lifelike. So often have we seen the grass green and the sky blue that we sometimes have wished, just once, to see the sky green and the grass blue, for then perhaps an artist's intention could be felt behind the whole thing.

Besides, colors in a film can never get to look completely like colors in nature. The reason is rather simple. In nature, the number of color shades are infinite. Even the human eye cannot distinguish them all from one another. It has been discovered that the greatest number of color shades that the human eye can perceive is 14,420. It is obvious that even the most sensitive color film can only reproduce a fraction of these 14,420 shades. So, on color film all the little color differences, the half-tones, are missing, all those that the eye perceives out in nature without seeing them. It is, on the whole, a mistake to approach color film with demands for naturalness. For there is nothing to prevent a film's colors from strongly deviating from those of nature and yet—or precisely therefore—give a richer artistic experience to the spectator.

For the director, the colors are a valuable aid. Carefully selected with consideration for their emotional affects and correctly weighed against each other, they can add an artistic quality to the film that it would not have had without the colors. To picture composition in the black-and-white film is added color composition in the color film. In the black-and-white film one works with light against darkness and with line against line; in the color film, with surface against surface, with form against form, and with color against color. What in the black-and-white picture is expressed through alternating light and shadow and the refraction of lines is now expressed in color constellations. To the many different rhythms that prevail in film is added the color rhythm. In color film, one must pay more attention to picture editing. The slightest shifting can mean a change of balance between the color surfaces, through which the harmony is broken. The film editing is all the more important in that not only the editing but also the pictorial composition, and with that the color composition, incessantly shift in the "flowing" pictures. This creates the effect of persons and objects being in constant motion and causes the colors to glide from one place to another in changing rhythms, creating new and surprising effects when they collide with other colors or melt into them. Incidentally, the general rule should be as few colors as possible, possibly combined with black and white colors, which are used much too little in these films. One has forgotten them in the childlike delight over the many more sparkling colors in the paintbox.

All of this makes the director's task more difficult but more tempting. Even in a black-and-white film, each scene must be conquered. The color does not make the conquest easier—but the victory more delicious when it is won. And even greater will the victory be when the director succeeds in breaking the vicious circle that still ties color film to black-and-white film's naturalistic preoccupations. The cinema has the possibility of becoming a great artistic experience—as far as color is concerned—only when it succeeds in entirely freeing itself from the embrace of naturalism. Only then do the colors have the possibility of expressing the unutterable, that which cannot be explained but only felt. Only then can colors help the feature film to get a foothold in the world of the abstract, which has been closed to it until now.

The director must not see his pictures in black-and-white and put on colors afterward. The pictures should emerge in colors before his inner eye. He must *create* in colors. However, a feeling for color isn't something that can be learned. Color is an optical experience, so the ability to see, think, and feel in colors must be innate. In general, I suppose one dare assume that it is mainly painters who possess this faculty. If the color film is not to continue its development in the same shameful way, so that only four or five artistic films in color can again be expected during the next twenty years, the film industry will probably have to accept assistance from those who can help—namely, from painters—just as one, with time, would bring oneself to secure help from poets, authors, composers, and ballet masters. The director of the color film should add to his already numerous staff of colleagues a painter, who, in collaboration with and under responsibility to the director, creates the color effects of the film. The painter should begin his task as early as possible so that the film's scenes may be conceived in colors and be born in the manuscript as colored sketches. A "color manuscript" must be established parallel to the basic manuscript, and the sketches must be elaborated in detail during further work until they end up as big, colored, live screens on the wall of the movie theatre.

One might object: "What does the director want with a painter? He has his color technicians, hasn't he?" There is no doubt that these advisors are and will continue to be of immense use to the director. With their experience and their knowledge of chromatology and color-theory they can save him from many pitfalls. But, with all due respect for their competence and sense of responsibility, the good painter has one good and important quality in preference to them, and it is for this quality's sake that he should be connected with the film: he is a *creating* artist himself. His impulses come from an artistic mind. And it will be an advantage to the color technicians to be associated with an expert, and they will in other respects be a necessary intermediary between him and the director—and the laboratory.

To make completely clear what is meant by the above, let us make a supposition. Let us imagine that Toulouse-Lautrec was alive and that he had collaborated on *Moulin Rouge* all through the film, right to the end, that is, not just during the opening scenes but also throughout the remainder of the picture. I wonder if then these later scenes would not have been at the same high level as the opening scene, which was based upon a color sketch by Toulouse-Lautrec himself. And wouldn't *Moulin Rouge,* then, instead of being a promising attempt, have become a truly great color film, a model in a time when the tendency is going in the direction of fewer and better films? And the director would not have received less credit for that reason, for it is not a director's task to do everything himself but to keep all of it together and force the many details into a compositional whole.

The wish that lies behind these lines is that color film will get out of the backwater it is in and sometime in the near future get to stand on its own feet. For the moment, it is drifting aimlessly, and when it is at its best it lives off loans. Usually, it doesn't set higher goals for itself than to "resemble." When it exerts itself, it takes pains to "resemble" something it is not—compare *Henry V,* which is supposed to "resemble" an illuminated manuscript from the Middle Ages and *Gate of Hell,* which is supposed to "resemble" old Japanese woodcuts. How refreshing it would be to see for once a color film that bears the stamp of a living artist from end to end. Then color film would become a real live art and not just colored film.

Imagination and Color (1955)

The whole question of color persisted in Dreyer's thinking throughout 1955. Several months after publishing the article on "Color Film and Colored Film," when he was called upon to prepare a lecture for the Edinburgh Film Festival, Dreyer expanded his thoughts on the relationship between color and imagination. Clearly, the prospect of working with color for the first time—something that was becoming increasingly likely and inevitable for him to do at long last—made Dreyer more immediately aware of new frontiers in the evolution of cinema. And so, as he worked his way toward the discussion of color occurring late in the lecture, Dreyer considered a number of issues related to artistic temperament, style, and experimentation.

Here, more clearly than anywhere else, he discusses the technique of "abstraction" that became the central problem and issue in his maturing aesthetic credo. The elusive point throughout his entire discussion of "new possibilities" is *newness*—primarily on grounds of *never having been fully realized.* He is explicit about this in his references to color, both in this article and the one preceding it. This is the major clue to the special wavelength of thought on which he develops his points. "Color" was in the foreground of his overall conception of *a cinema of the imagination* because he had seen color so thoroughly plundered by the manufacturers of *usable* films, rather than explored and brought to full flower artistically. To Dreyer, therefore, the question of color reopens the larger issue of a general re-evaluation of how far cinema had come, of how many casually and exploitatively used potentialities of cinema might be deepened and refined. And so he makes his basic point once more: For the artist, film cannot be mere reportage. A work of the imagination goes beyond the direct recording of the newsreel. But how far? How far would Dreyer carry this type of formalism? He has told us how he would play with color. What else would he do? Two things, at least, from what he says here. Holding only the organic or architectonic principle inviolable—something made plain in his analogy between the film director and the architect—Dreyer outlines a daring experiment: we know that *abstraction* can be applied to color, but why not to basic film space? Why not, Dreyer suggests, eliminate illusionistic depth of field—one of the apparent "absolutes" of the two-dimensional screen? The results would have to be seen, but the very notion suggests the closeness between Dreyer and present-day experimental filmmakers who are preoccupied with the problem and implications of illusionism. Awareness of the experimental dynamic at work in each of Dreyer's films—each an experiment in its own right, as he has told us—will perhaps bring us closer to the unique and fresh vision he arrives at, rather than confusing the delicacy of his balance with somewhat reminiscent, stock usages. As Peter Kubelka, the Austrian experimental film artist has observed in an interview with the editor: "The fact that *Gertrud* meets so much resistance is that it is a film of absolute newness and it belongs to the outposts of the avant-garde, although it doesn't seem so. Although the film has a conventional aspect, it is something never seen before."

And, of course, nothing typifies this more than the apparently simple *rooms* in Dreyer's films. He will develop the point in the article about to follow. But when he talks about the "soul of a room," recall the vivified space of the nearly empty chambers that Joan of Arc spent her final hours in; the "haunted" enclosures of *Vampyr;* and the households of *Day of Wrath, Ordet,* and *Gertrud,* all differentiated, each vibrating with the special life Dreyer has given it.

Here, then, is a transcript of the Edinburgh lecture of August 29, 1955.

I think we can all agree that film, as it is today, is not perfect. For this, we should be only grateful, because in the imperfect there is continuing development. The imperfect is alive. The perfect is dead, set aside, we give it little attention. But in the imperfect a thousand possibilities break through.

Film as an art is right now in a period of upheaval, and one scans the horizon to discover where the new impulses will come from.

Of course, by now you are expecting a long, profound lecture with learned analyses and that sort of thing, but I must disappoint you. I am not a film theorist—I don't have the brains for that. I am only a film director who is proud of his craft. But even a craftsman has his thoughts during work, and it is these simple reflections that I am going to share with you.

There is nothing revolutionary in what I have to tell you. I don't believe in revolutions. They have, as a rule, the tedious quality of pulling development back. I believe more in evolution, in the small advances. And so it is my intention to point only to the possibilities the film has for an artistic renewal *from within*.

Human beings follow the law of inertia and resist being led away from the beaten track. They have become accustomed to precise, photographic reproduction of reality now, and they probably feel a certain pleasure in seeing again what they already know. When the camera appeared in its time, it won a quick victory with its ability to register objectively by mechanical means the visual impressions of the human eye. This ability has until now been the strength of cinema, but with regard to artistic films it is becoming a weakness that we shall have to combat. We have been hung up on photography and are faced with the necessity of freeing ourselves from it. We must use the camera to supersede the camera. We must work toward no longer being slaves of photography but becoming masters of it. Photography must be transformed from being used for purely reporting and become a tool for artistic inspiration; the business of direct observation should be handed over to the sight-seeing sections of the newsreels.

Reportorial photography has compelled cinema to keep down to earth, so that it has become addicted to naturalism. Only after it cuts these moorings will cinema have the possibility of rising to the heights of imagination. Therefore, we must wrest cinema away from the embrace of naturalism. We must get it into our heads that it is only a waste of time to copy reality. We must give cinema a new artistic form and create a new stylistic language with the aid of the camera. But first we must realize what we mean by the concepts "art" and "style." The Danish author, Johannes V. Jensen describes "art" as "soulfully composed form." That is a definition which is simple and very much to the point. The same goes for the definition the English philosopher Chesterfield gives to the concept of "style." He says: "Style is the dress of thoughts." This is right, provided that "the dress" is not too conspicuous, for a characteristic of good style must be that it enters into such an intimate bond with matter that it is absorbed into a higher unity with it. If it imposes and strikes the eye, it is no longer "style" but "manner." I will define "style" myself as "the form in which the artistic inspiration expresses itself," for, as you know, one recognizes an artist's style by certain features, peculiar to him, which reflect his mind and personality in his work.

Style in an artistic film is the resultant of many different components such as the play of rhythms and lines, the mutual tension of color surfaces, the interaction of light and shadow, the camera's gliding rhythms—all of which, together with the director's interpretation of the material as an image-generating factor, is decisive for his artistic form of expression—his style! If he confines himself to a soulless, impersonal copy of what his eyes are seeing, he has no style. But if he, in his mind, takes what he sees and works it into a vision, and if he builds up the images of the film in accordance with this vision, regardless of the reality that inspired him, then his work will bear the holy stamp of inspiration—then the film will have style, for style is the imprint of personality in the work.

I admit that is sounds very immodest, but on behalf of myself and other directors I now venture to assert that it is the director who must and shall leave his mark on the artistic film. In this lies no failure to appreciate the writer's share, but, even if the writer is Shakespeare himself, a literary idea in itself does not turn a film into a work of art. It happens only when a director, inspired by the writer's material, in a convincing way gives it life in artistic images. Nor do I underestimate the teamwork performed by photographers, color technicians, and architects, etc., but within this collective, the director is and always will be—and has to be—the driving and inspiring force. He is the man behind the work. It is he who makes the poet's word resound so that we listen, it is he who makes feelings and passions blaze so that we are gripped and moved. It is he who stamps the film with this inexplicable something that is called style.

Well, so this is my opinion of a director's importance—and *responsibility*. In any case, we now realize what film style is. But we should also like to know what an artistic film is. Let us formulate the question like this: What other branch of art is most adjacent to the film? In my opinion it must be architecture. The distinctive mark of distinguished architecture is that all details are so finely attuned to the whole that no part, not even the smallest, can be altered without it being felt as a flaw in the entirety—as opposed to the nonarchitectural house where all measurements and proportions are accidental. Something similar is true of cinema. Only when all the artistic elements a film consists of are welded together into a firmly built composition, so that none of its components can be omitted or changed without the entirety suffering from it, only then can film be compared to an architectonic work of art, and all the films that do not satisfy these strict demands are then merely like dull and conventional houses that we pass by indifferently. In the architectonic film it is the director who takes over the role of the architect. It is he who, from his artistic outlook, coordinates the multifarious rhythms and tensions of the film with the dramatic curves of the written work and the psychological vibrations in the actors' facial expressions and exchanges of words—and, thus, imprints his style on the film.

And now we come to the real question, namely: Where does the possibility of an artistic renewal of film lie? I, for my part, can see only one way: *abstraction*—but, in order not to be misunderstood, I hurry to define the word "abstraction" as an expression for the perception of art which demands that an artist shall abstract from reality in order to reinforce its spiritual content, whether this is of psychological or purely aesthetic nature. Or said even more succinctly: Art shall represent the *inner* and not the *outer* life. Therefore, we must get away from naturalism and find alternatives in order to introduce abstraction in our pictures. The ability to abstract is the prerequisite. Abstraction gives the director a possibility to reach outside the fence behind which naturalism has enclosed the film. Cinema must work itself away from being a purely imitative art. The ambitious director must seek a higher reality than the one he obtains just by putting his camera up and copying reality. His pictures have to be not only a visual but also a spiritual experience. What is important is that the director share his own artistic and spiritual experiences with the audience, and abstraction gives him this possibility by allowing the director to replace objective reality with his own subjective perceptions.

But if abstraction is to be introduced into cinema, we must begin by discovering the new creative principles. Let me stress that I only have *the image* in mind today. But this is only reasonable, for people think in images, and in film the image is the primary thing.

I am going to point out some of the paths that stand open for the director who wants to introduce the abstract element into his pictures. To name the most obvious: *simplification*. This is the task of any creative artist: To let himself be inspired by reality and after that withdraw from it in order to give the work the form that the inspiration suggested to him. Therefore, the director must have the liberty to transform reality so that it will correspond to the inspired, simplified scene he has standing in his consciousness, for it is not the director's aesthetic sense that should yield to reality—no, the opposite: reality should obey his aesthetic sense. For art is not imitation but subjective selection, and so the director will include only what is necessary for a clear and spontaneous overall effect.

The simplification should also aim at making the idea of the image more explicit and clear. Thus, the simplification must consist in purifying the motif of whatever doesn't support the idea: But by this simplification the motif is transformed into a symbol,

SIMPLIFICATION. *Day of Wrath*. ". . . only what is necessary for a clear and spontaneous overall effect."

SIMPLIFICATION. *Ordet*. ". . . true—but purged of trivial details."

SIMPLIFICATION. *Gertrud*. Nina Pens Rode. ". . . the spirit in and behind things."

SIMPLIFICATION. Carl Dreyer on the set of *Gertrud*.

and with symbolism we are already in abstraction, for the idea of symbolism is to operate through suggestion.

The cinematic representation of reality should be true, but purged of trivial details. It should also be realistic, but transformed in the director's mind in such a way that it becomes poetry. It is not the things in reality that the director should be interested in but, rather, the spirit in and behind the things. For realism is in itself not art. The realities must be forced into a form of simplification and abbreviation and in a purified state reappear in a kind of timeless psychological realism.

This abstraction through a simplification and an inspired selection of things can even be put into practice by the director, in a modest way, in the film's rooms themselves. How many soulless rooms have we not seen in film? The director can give soul to his rooms through a simplification whereby he removes all superfluous things to the advantage of the few objects that, in one way or another, have value as psychological evidence of the occupant's personality or characterize his relation to the idea of the film.

A much, much more important means for abstraction is, of course, *colors*. With them, everything is possible—although not before we succeed in breaking the chain that still binds the color film to the photographic naturalism of the black-and-white film. Just as the French impressionists were inspired by classical Japanese woodcut artists, in a similar way there is every possible reason for Western film directors to learn from the Japanese film, *Gate of Hell,* where the colors really serve their purpose. I would think that the Japanese themselves regard this film as a naturalistic film, in historical costumes, of course, but still naturalistic. Seen with our eyes, however, it seems like a stylized film with attempts at the abstract. Only in one single sequence does pure naturalism break through, namely in the scenes of the tournament on the open green plain. For a few minutes the style is broken, but one's displeasure with this is quickly forgotten through the beauty the rest of the film gives us. There is certainly no doubt that the colors were chosen according to a careful, preconceived plan. In any case, this film tells us quite a bit, not only about the color composition and the well-known rhythm of the classical Japanese woodcuts but also about the grouping of warm and cold colors—and about the use of extensive simplification, which has a particularly strong effect here because it is supported by the colors.

Gate of Hell should encourage Western directors to use colors more purposefully and also with greater boldness and imagination. So far, the colors in the majority of Western films have been used much too casually and in accordance with the naturalistic recipe. At the moment, we are pussyfooting. When it is a real wild affair, we throw ourselves into pastel shades to show that we do, after all, have some taste. But when it comes to the abstract color film, having taste isn't enough; one must have artistic intuition and the courage to choose exactly the colors that support the dramatic and psychological content of the film. In the colors lies the great, yes, the very greatest possibility for a renewal of the artistic resources of cinema, so let us by all means learn from the Japanese. Others have done this before us—among them, the famous American painter, James Whistler.

While I am talking about the colors, which in themselves, of course, contain unlimited possibilities for abstraction, there is another phenomenon worth mentioning because it might possibly inspire an abstraction of a very special sort. As is well known, the photograph presumes an atmospheric perspective, which means that the contrast between light and shadow diminishes into the background. Perhaps there is an idea for an interesting abstraction in the conscious elimination of the atmospheric perspective—or, in other words, by giving up the much-coveted illusion of depth and distance. Instead, one could work toward an entirely new image construct of color surfaces, all on the same plane, forming one great, aggregated surface of many colors from which the notion of foreground, middleground, and background would be completely dropped. In other words, one could move away from the perspectivistic picture and pass on to pure surface effect. It is possible that by taking this direction we might obtain quite singular aesthetic effects, just right for film.

I hope I haven't made you nervous with all this talk about "abstraction." I guess to film people's ears it is almost a bad word. The purpose of what I have said here today has, however, been only to draw attention to the fact that there is a world outside the grayness and tedium of naturalism, namely: the world of the imagination. Of course, this conversion must take place without the director and his collaborators losing their foothold in the world of realities. Even though he must make reality the object of an artistic transformation, the transformed reality must, however, be rendered so that the viewer recognizes it and believes in it. It is altogether of importance that the first attempts at introducing abstraction in cinema be done with tact and discretion, so as not to shock. It would be wise to lead the audience slowly into the new paths. But if the experiments are successful, huge new expanses will open up to cinema. No task will be too great. Perhaps cinema will never become really three-dimensional, but with the help of abstraction it will, on the other hand, be possible to introduce both a fourth and fifth dimension in cinema.

In the end, just this: I have talked much about image and form and not a word about actors, but anyone who has seen my films—the good ones—will know what great importance I attach to the actors' work. There is nothing in the world that can be compared to the human face. It is a land one never becomes tired of exploring, a land with a beauty of its own, whether rough or gentle. There is no greater experience than that of witnessing, in the studio, the expression in a sensitive face becoming animated from within and, under the mysterious power of inspiration, growing into poetry.

The Roots of Anti-Semitism (1959)

As a Dane in Occupied Denmark during World War II, Dreyer must have been keenly aware of the persecution of the Jews by the Nazis-in-residence and just across the border in Germany itself. And, of course, the help the Danes themselves gave to Jews in hiding or escaping is one of the more impressive legends emerging from World War II. In writing about anti-Semitism, however, Dreyer strikes an even deeper personal chord. Eight years earlier, in 1951, in the same journal, *Politiken,* he had treated the question: "Who Killed Jesus?" If one looks at Dreyer's filmmaking, from the very beginning—as early as *The President* (1920), for that matter—the theme of false accusation runs regularly through his work, resulting in some of his most powerfully felt motion pictures. This thematic concern is perhaps even more germane than the specific treatment of anti-Semitism in Dreyer's 1922 film, *Die Gezeichneten* (Love One Another). Both *Joan of Arc* and *Day of Wrath* involve victimizations based upon backward or erroneous—certainly, *irrational*—assumptions. The careful tracing of anti-Semitism's evolution from the earliest moments of the Christian epoch makes the essay to follow a model of Dreyer's preoccupation with the problem. His central motive, once again, appears to be *de*mystification of the religious experience, not to reduce it to the routine or undermine its grandeur but to unify it with life on earth. This can be seen in the way Dreyer describes Paul's role in the propagation of Christianity and the emergence of anti-Semitism:

Jesus becomes an unknown man whose divine qualities appear only when he rises from the dead on the third day. And, of course, it wasn't on the Romans' own initiative that he was nailed to the cross, no—it happened at the explicit request of the high priests and the scribes. Paul has closed his eyes and ears to this "pious" delusion, which took it out on the orthodox Jews and still does to this day.

Dreyer wrote this essay just halfway through the decade that elapsed between *Ordet* (1954) and *Gertrud* (1964). It appeared in *Politiken*, October 31, 1959. Throughout this period, his primary hopes were for making the Jesus film.

The painfully scrupulous and conscientious official, Rudolf Höss, whose autobiography, *Commandant of Auschwitz*, has recently been published in Danish, was in 1941 called to a meeting with Heinrich Himmler, who informed him that "der Führer" had decided on a "final solution" of the Jewish question and that Himmler, for his part, had decided to entrust the execution of the plan to Mr. Höss.

With these instructions, Mr. Höss went back to Auschwitz. After having undertaken certain calculations, he ordered four crematories, with furnaces and gas chambers attached, from the company of Topf und Söhne, of Erfurt, for installation "soonest possible."

The four crematories were capable of burning 12,000 bodies per day, so that it was therefore possible to burn 4,380,000 bodies a year. However, during the period May to August, 1944, even these four furnaces could not satisfy the need, so certain shipments of Hungarian Jews had to be executed by means of pyres in the open air. It is in this way that, in August of 1944, one reaches the considerable number of 24,000 cremations in a single day.

In his autobiography, Höss writes the following: "I should like to mention that I, for my part, have never harbored any hateful feelings toward the Jews. To feel hatred is entirely alien to me."

When one's nausea has subsided, you take your head in your hands and ask: How did anti-Semitism ever come into this world, after all? What is its origin, its background?

In order to find answers to these questions, we must go back rather more than nineteen hundred years in time. Back to Golgotha. Here, too, Jews were done away with. One of them was the Jew, Jesus. For him, too, a "final solution" was found—at least they thought so then, the Romans.

That Jesus was crucified was not a result of anti-Semitism. The concept was not yet invented. No, Jesus died on the cross as a political rebel. His followers spread his doctrine and the little fraternal community developed into a sect that was named the Nazarenes. It is worth noting that it was not a *Christian* sect but a *Jewish* one. Christianity as a theological concept did not yet exist. The members of the sect were all Jews who observed the Jews' law, the Torah, and complied with all the ceremonial precepts.

Then some rather dramatic events took place within the sect which were to become of decisive importance to its future. Seven Hellenistic Jews who had come to Jerusalem were admitted to the sect. One of them, Stephen, one day appeared in a Jerusalem synagogue and entered a dispute with some Pharisees, before whom he praised the crucified Jesus at the expense of the clergy. Some Jews, loyal to the temple, lodged a complaint against Stephen with the Jewish council. One of these temple-loyals was, according to what is maintained, a tentmaker by the name of Saul (from Tarsus). He is also said to have been present when Stephen was taken outside the town and stoned.

Saul was young, so it is possible this was the first time he attended a murder by stoning, and since he, with his impulsive temperament, hardly could have restricted himself to being a passive spectator, it is probable that the stoning brought about a crisis of remorse within him that psychologically explains the "heavenly vision" he encountered on his way to Damascus. Jesus appeared before him and called to him: "Saul, Saul, why are you persecuting me?" He fell to the ground and was stricken with blindness. Only on the third day thereafter did he regain his sight. A man of the Nazarene's sect opened his eyes and admonished him not to be *against* but *for* the new faith. After a great spiritual struggle Saul decided to join the Nazarenes.

At a very early moment, it seems to have been clear to Saul that if the Nazarenes were not to remain a small Jewish sect that would sooner or later disintegrate and crumble away for want of increase, they had to take up new attitudes. From where could they expect an influx if not among the heathens outside Palestine and, especially, within the borders of the extensive Roman Empire? But such a task could be solved only by a Hellenistic Jew who spoke Hebrew as well as Greek and who was familiar with the heathen peoples' attitude toward religion and ethics—a preacher and agitator. Saul knew a man who was equal to the task. Saul was the man's name, but he would soon change his name to Paul. At the same time, he appointed himself an apostle. He was called to Antioch where he had many followers. These did not wish to be called Nazarenes and chose to call themselves Christians. It is the first time we meet this designation. The Christian community decided some time later to send Paul on a missionary journey to the surrounding heathen countries, and Paul, thereby, had his highest hopes fulfilled.

But what was Paul's first impression of the foreign milieu? I wonder if he was not, first and foremost, surprised at the large number of Jews he came across? The explanation was that the majority of the Jewish people did not live in Palestine, but outside: one estimates—in Palestine, three million, and outside, three and a half million—of these, of course, the vast majority within the Roman Empire and its provinces in Europe, Asia Minor, Egypt, and North Africa. These Jews had their own synagogues in most towns. The Jews abroad felt strongly attached to their faith, on the whole, and, through this, also to Jerusalem and the Temple, which was the religious center for all Jews—wherever they lived in the world. The Jews outside Palestine not only adhered to their faith but, encouraged by the clergy in Jerusalem, they made intense propaganda in the time before and after Jesus to gain ground among the heathens, and not without success. That so many heathens found their way into Jewry was due to the fact, partly, that there was respect for the Jewish faith and, partly, that a certain religious ferment prevailed among the heathens themselves. The prestige of the old gods and goddesses was on the decline. Nobody took them seriously anymore. Together with this contempt for the gods, an unconscious longing for a new faith that gave guarantees for the

From *Die Gezeichneten*. Richard Boleslawski as Fedja in Dreyer's early film about anti-Semitism.

future grew up among enlightened heathens. Undoubtedly contributing to this were the Stoics, whose philosophy prepared the ground for Christianity, as their thoughts lay close to the principal ideas in the Christian doctrine. Thus Posidonius had come so far that he believed in only one God "who is within us, in our hearts."

In any case, the path was open for Paul and his new religion. He realized that Christianity's great chance was in the fact that it satisfied a burning need of the time. Therefore, it was a question of striking while the iron was hot. The heathens were hungering for a new religion, but preferably one that did not make life too difficult. The Jewish faith in its most demanding form required the observance of no less than 613 commandments (which even Jews by birth had some difficulties observing). What did Paul do? He simply let the requirement of believing in Jesus replace the 613 commandments—then there were no more problems on that score. Along with the 613 commandments, rules about circumcision and the eating-ban were dropped. Paul wanted to make his Christianity an easier thing, both for the one hundred percent heathens and for the half-Jews, and—seen with Jewish eyes—one dare say that he probably succeeded to perfection. For Christianity, Paul retained only two practices: Baptism and the community meal.

The Jews who in their hearts had remained faithful to the ancestral religion were naturally deeply offended at the loose morals with which Paul disposed of religious questions that to them were of the very greatest importance. Had not Jesus himself said: "Do not think that I have come to destroy the law. I do not come to destroy but to fulfill." But what does Paul do? He sweeps away the whole law!

It is understandable that Paul's behavior awakens the righteous indignation of the orthodox Jews, to such a degree sometimes that they unite and chase him from their town.

It is strange, however, that although Paul's new faith deviates more and more from the true Jewish doctrine, Paul still considers himself a Jew, something he also is—by birth and by conviction. According to his own opinion, the faith that he is preaching is in reality Judaism in a new, simplified form. He himself loyally and conscientiously obeys the ceremonial laws, but he doesn't want to

demand of others that they subject themselves to what he considers
an absurd and superfluous formality.

It could be tempting to follow Paul to the bitter end of his
martyrdom but that is not the purpose of this essay. However, as
a final vignette, I want to mention the precise characterization that
the Jewish historian, Joseph Klausner, gives of the apostle to the
heathens. "Paul," he says,

> had transformed a little Jewish sect into a half-Jewish, half-Christian
> religion that spread over the whole world. He was *the real founder of
> Christianity*. It can safely be said: without Jesus, no Paul. But it can
> be said with equal confidence: without Paul, no Christian world reli-
> gion with a clearly developed and easily understandable theology.

Before we completely leave Paul, we must leaf through a little
bit of the Acts of the Apostles—at least the part that deals with
Paul. It is believed to have been written by the Greek-Christian,
Luke, the author of the Gospel According to St. Luke, a close
friend of Paul. What immediately strikes one when reading it is
the hostile tendency toward the Jews. In twenty places, the Jews
are mentioned in a hateful way. Apparently, according to this
document, the Jews are the source of everything evil. They perse-
cute the Christians and try to hurt them by slandering them before
the Romans. Many things indicate that Paul has inspired Luke to
these underhanded attacks on the Jews. If this is the case, we con-
front a most peculiar phenomenon, namely: the anti-Semitic Jew.

Some Bible critics have a plausible explanation for the phenomenon. Paul does, they think, through intuition get hold of the right
end of a great religious idea. Being the outstanding agitator that
he is, he hammers away and builds it up. The heathens rally
around him. One Christian community after another springs up.
Soon he sits at the center of a big web and needs only to pull the
strings.

There are, however, a couple of dangerous rocks he must try to
steer around. One is the orthodox Jews, who consider him a
bungler. The other is the Romans, who don't place obstacles in
his way. Paul, of whom it was said that his "heart did not resemble his face," knows how to talk for the Romans so they get con-

From *Die Gezeichneten*.

fidence both in him and the doctrine he spreads. Now Paul does not, of course, loudly proclaim that the Jesus the heathens are urged to kneel for is the same that the Romans, years ago, crucified on Golgotha for rebellious attempts against the Roman occupying power. Jesus becomes an unknown man whose divine qualities appear only when he rises from the dead on the third day. And, of course, it wasn't on the Romans' own initiative that he was nailed to the cross, no—it happened at the explicit request of the high priests and the scribes. Paul has closed his eyes and ears to this "pious" delusion, which took it out on the orthodox Jews and still does to this day. Fanatics of Paul's kind seldom have any scruples when it comes to promoting the cause for which they are fighting. So much for the Bible critics.

The Acts of the Apostles, composed in its final form, is supposed to be from approximately the year 95, after the birth of Christ. The Crucifixion took place in the year 30, and in the year 70 the Temple was leveled to the ground, Jerusalem conquered by the Romans, and the Jewish inhabitants of the city sold as slaves. The Jews as a nation and as a people sank deeper and deeper, and when the account of Paul came into existence, they were completely without importance and could not protest, while the Romans stood at the height of their power.

Perhaps without thinking of the consequences, *Paul sowed the first seeds of the Christian anti-Semitism,* which even during the first days of the Roman church would grow up and spread like dangerous weeds. The inclination to fawn upon the Romans and to smear the Jews also appears in the Gospel According to St. John, which is from the same period as the Acts of the Apostles (i.e., toward the end of the first century) and shows the same hostile tendency toward the Jews.

Two things are striking in a reading of this Gospel. First of all, the word "Jew" is found much more often than in the three other Gospels. While the word appears five times in Luke and Matthew and six times in Mark, it figures in John—seventy times. Next, John talks about the Jews as if he were talking about a foreign people—foreign to Jesus and foreign to himself, and always in a scornful or contemptuous way.

The explanation is probably the same as in the case of Paul, namely, the consideration for the Romans who were right on top of him and with whom he was interested in being on good terms— unless a transcriber has independently made corrections in the manuscript in order not to get the evangelist (and himself) into trouble.

Some years ago a book, *Jésus et Israel,* was published in French by the Jewish historian living in Paris, Jules Isaac. Jules Isaac, personally, has been at such close quarters with the German anti-Semitism that it still pains him to think of it. On the first page of the book, one reads the following lines:

> To my wife and my daughter
> killed by the Germans
> killed
> Simply because their name was Isaac.

In his book, Jules Isaac points out how Christendom has for centuries on continued to bring fertilizer to the ghastly weeds of anti-Semitism.

A schematic arrangement will give easier general view:

Second century; the holy Justin: "Your circumcision is the mark of infamy with which omniscient providence has beforehand stamped you the murderers of Jesus and the prophets."

Third century; the theologian and Bible interpreter, Origines: "It is the Jews who nailed Jesus to the cross."

Fourth century; the church historian, Bishop of Caesarea: "Thus the Jews were chastised as a punishment for their crime and their impiety."

The holy Ephrem calls the Jews "circumcised dogs."

Church Father Jeronimus stamps the Jews as "snakes in Judas' image" and solemnly promises them the Christians' hatred.

The holy John Chrysostomos: "How can it be that believing Christians are not ashamed of having contact with those who have shed the blood of Jesus?"

Fifth century; the holy Augustinus: "The final hour has come for our Lord, Jesus! They hold him—the Jews. They insult him— the Jews. They bind him—the Jews. They crown him with thorns, they soil him with their spittle, they whip him, they shower him with scorn, they nail him to the cross, they plunge their lances into his flesh."

Right through the Middle Ages the Catholic Fathers fertilize the seeds of hatred for the Jews. Then the reformers come to their aid. *Luther* declares that if he finds a pious Jew to baptize he will bring him out on the bridge over the Elbe, bind him, fasten a stone around his neck, and throw him into the river with the words: I baptize you in the name of Abraham!

Luther can put his arm around the Catholic Fathers. Each and every one of them must bear his part of the responsibility that Anne Frank had to die. But let us not thump our chest and believe that our own time is better. What do you think, for instance, of a little "legend" that Papini has written and that is about a high-ranking Jewish rabbi who goes to the Pope to make a deal with him. The rabbi offers that a very great number of Jews will christen themselves if the Church will, in return, strike the Passion Week from its calendar. In addition, the rabbi offers a mountain of gold. The Pope answers with sublime dignity: "Do not force me to say that a Judas lives within every Jew. You sold Jesus for thirty pieces of silver and today you want to buy him back with some of the gold you have hoarded over the course of centuries through pillage and usury." This legend is from 1938.

Eight years later (1946), Daniel Rops wrote in his holy story about Jesus: "The Jews had shouted: Let his blood come over us and our children. God in his righteousness heard them." And he continues: "The face of persecuted Israel fills history but it does not make us forget that other face, soiled with blood and spittle—this other face for which the Jews felt no pity."

Finally, from Herbert Pundik's little book on "Israel 1948–1958," I take the following little footnote:

On the 26th of June, 1947, the English Comander-in-Chief in Palestine, Sir Evelyn Barker, sent out an army order in which he forbade the English troops to fraternize with the Jews in Palestine. The army order ended with the words: "I understand that these measures will create difficulties for the soldiers (but) they will punish the Jews ex-

From *Die Gezeichneten.*

actly in the way that this race hates more than anything else: by aiming a blow against their pockets and showing them how much we detest them."

Now, for nineteen hundred years the Jews have been held responsible for Jesus' death and have been stamped murderers—Christ-killers. The curse has followed them, hatred has been preached against them, and they have been tortured and murdered in multitudes. This has to stop some time, after all. The Christians' aversion against the Jews is foolish and illogical. Think of what the Christians have received from the Jews; above all, the faith in one God who is God of both Christian and Jew. Next, the idea that all human beings are equal to God. Christianity is a child of Judaism and the New Testament has its roots in Jewish tradition. Christian eyes must be opened to the mutual connection between Jewish faith and Christian faith and Jewish and Christian ethics. Only through mutual understanding leading to mutual respect and sympathy, only in this and not in anything else can one see a "final solution"—as blessed Adolf once put it.

Ebbe Neergaard (1960)

Ebbe Neergaard was Denmark's greatest film critic and historian. Dreyer wrote the short piece appearing below as a commemorative preface to Neergaard's *The Story of the Danish Film,* a critical history published posthumously in 1960.

Neergaard was born in 1901. He taught English and German literature at the University of Berlin between 1928 and 1933. From 1933 to 1940 he was the headmaster of a school in Denmark, but in the forties became a film critic for *Extrabladet* and *Information. A Film Director's Work,* his monograph on Dreyer, was first published in 1940 and later updated for the British Film Institute's edition in 1963. It is still a valuable contribution toward the understanding of Dreyer and the origins of many of its insights are reflected upon by Dreyer in the deeply personal eulogy that follows.

Well, my dear Neergaard, so this time it is *I* who will write about *you.* For a change. You know I do it gladly, as small part-payment of the debt I owe you.

And what shall I then tell? That you always have been quite a bit ahead of the vanguard of film? You were among the very first who saw a new art form in the film. You also were among the first who maintained that the art of cinema was different from that of the theatre, that cinema had other artistic laws. Cinema should be neither theatre nor literature. As one of the first, you demanded a *cinematic* film. Yes, I could reel off a long list of phenomena in connection with the evolution of cinema that nobody before you had caught sight of. Much of what you said and wrote then seems obvious to us today but it was not so at that time.

I know you don't care for eulogies, so let me rather refresh some memories of Paris. I had finished *Joan of Arc* at the time and was preparing *Vampyr*. Mrs. Beate was in England visiting friends, so we two film fanatics had the long evenings to ourselves. Maybe we also went to the movies and afterward ate at Chez Père Louis. Ate and talked! About what? About film, of course—what else? And mostly about *Joan of Arc*. You could like it because—as you put it—it broke away from habitual professional thinking. We also discussed Falconetti's performance as Joan of Arc. We talked for quite a while about the remarkable thing that happened when an actress like Falconetti, in her inspired moments, from a hiding place within, brought out feelings that were strange to her and that she herself didn't know she had. We talked about how wonderful must it not be for her, the next day, when the footage was shown to her, to then see her own face a glow of inspired, almost supernatural beauty? What was it that happened in Falconetti's core during such filming? She could not explain it herself, so we ended up describing this mysterious something as a secret that, by its very nature, should be experienced and not explained. Maybe it was right that an actor can understand another human being only when he has that other human being—*and also its opposite*—in himself. This explains, in any case, how Falconetti, who at night shone in the lighter dramatic art of the boulevard theatres, in the morning found completely sublime expressions for what Joan felt when her life was about to run out.

At a time when film had not yet disengaged itself from the theatre, you demanded that, on film, the actor must forget that he is an actor. Falconetti fulfilled this demand. She *lived* the part of Joan of Arc. It was clear that she had Joan in her. In her good moments there was something indefinable about her—something that was not of this world.

Naturally, we talked about other things besides *Joan of Arc*. One evening we discussed Stanislavski and his theories. I remember that I found it exaggerated and somewhat farfetched that Stanislavski demanded of an actor who was to play a conservative

GENERATING THE FIELD. Dreyer on the set of *Gertrud* with Axel Strøbye and Nina Pens Rode. The Dreyer Experience.

GENERATING THE FIELD. Dreyer directing a player for the documentary, *They Caught the Ferry* (1948). The Dreyer Touch.

GENERATING THE FIELD. Birgitte Federspiel being directed by Dreyer in *Ordet*. The Dreyer Secret? Photograph courtesy The Museum of Modern Art Film Stills Archive, New York.

bureaucrat that he cancel the subscription to the liberal newspaper he read every day and, instead, take out a subscription to a conservative paper with the obligation to read the same. "No," you said categorically, "Stanislavski is right. Three months reading the conservative paper would probably bring about a change of mentality in the spirit of the role." And in support of your assertion you stated that Pascal had once said that he, within a short period, would undertake to convert the worst heathen into a pious man— if the man could be persuaded to go to church three times each day to kneel, say a prayer, make the sign of the cross, put a coin in the church box, and sprinkle himself with holy water—and of course go to confession and appear at the service.

We also got to talk about *Vampyr,* which I was to start on. You gave me a good piece of advice, which I made a mental note of. "Remember," you said, "this thing that 'the photo does not lie' is nonsense. The photo lies for good reason if one wants it to do so. Only, directors haven't yet learned to make it lie in such a way that a style comes out of it." I really think that your advice gave me the courage to venture out further than I originally intended to in *Vampyr.* Having you behind me gave me confidence.

Personally, I am grateful to you because you again and again offered the opinion that a director must be regarded as a creative artist and that it is he who is responsible for the film as a cinematic work of art. It is the director's personality that stamps the film—or to use your own words: it does not depend so much on the *subject* as on the *form* the director gives it, because it is the director who creates the film and has the responsibility for it as a work of art. These, at that time, were words that spoke directly to my heart—and they still are.

Dear Neergaard, we are many, from many countries who miss you for your belief in and fresh outlook on cinema and for your willingness to find new ways that lead upward, up to the heights, to the wide open spaces where, in film, too—truth and beauty meet and become poetry.